About the Author

Warwick Broadhurst is a former pig hunter and animal control officer who now lives in retirement with his wife Jill.

I dedicate this book to my children and grandchildren.

Thank you to my friends Daniel Robin, Maurie Smith, and John Whiting, for contributing photos, and to Adam Nisbett for his artwork. Thank you to Rosemary Morton for her patient help with the proofreading. A special thank you to Graham Gurr of Halcyon Publishing for his kind advice, and also to Ian Wishart and Bozidar Jokanovic of Howling At The Moon Publishing for the editing, design and production of this book. Thanks also to all my pig hunting friends who hunted with me, and made this all possible. Finally thanks to my wife Jill, for her patience in typing the manuscript, and for her determination to complete this work, and to my very good friend Peter Robin who doggedly encouraged me to complete this task.

Porkers

Warwick Broadhurst

BROADHURST PUBLISHING

Broadhurst Publishing

First edition published 2015
by Broadhurst Publishing
2/82 Maidstone Road
Ilam
Christchurch 8041, NEW ZEALAND

Email: broadhurstpublishing@gmail.com

Copyright © Warwick Broadhurst, 2015
Copyright © Broadhurst Publishing Ltd, 2015

The moral rights of the author have been asserted.

Porkers is copyright. Except for the purpose of fair reviewing, no part of this publication may be copied, reproduced or transmitted in any form or by any means, including via technology either already in existence or developed subsequent to publication, without the express written permission of the publisher and authors. All rights reserved.

ISBN 978-0-473-31667-9 (PRINT), ISBN 978-0-473-31668-6 (KINDLE)

Cover photo of Warwick and pig by Geoff Mills/background by Newscom
Cartoons in text by Adam Nisbett
Typeset in Adobe Garamond Pro and Helvetica Neue
Cover concept: Heidi and Ian Wishart, and Bozidar Jokanovic
Book design: Bozidar Jokanovic

Contents

Introduction 6
Beginnings 8
The Cora Lynn Ripper 23
Murchison Pigs 35
Choose Your Companions Carefully 51
Woodchester 66
Accidents and Mishaps 76
Lessons Learned 98
Island Hills 107
Hunting on Forestry Land 127
Old Jack Barker 137
Tame Wild Pigs 146
Good Dogs I Have Known 168
Early Memories 182

Introduction

THIS BOOK WAS WRITTEN IN response to the many friends who have enjoyed my tales and kept telling me I should write a book! But primarily I wrote it for my children and grandchildren to give them an insight and a record of the adventures encountered by myself and my hunting companions in the early days.

Hunting is an age-old pursuit of man. While we do not need to hunt for our food in these modern times, the sport of hunting fulfils an inbuilt instinct for some. It is also an eco-friendly method of pest control that doesn't involve toxic poisons, and where carcasses are removed and put to good use. While deer stalking is one way, I never found it as exciting as hunting pigs with the dogs.

In addition to harming native bush and farm paddocks, pigs often attack and eat other animals, such as lambs and other vulnerable young.

Hunters will go anywhere there is the slightest chance of getting a pig and love exploring new country. Getting up before the sun, smelling the clean fresh dew on the grasses, the pride of the dogs getting a big boar, the thrill of the chase, heart racing, lungs nearly bursting while trying to hold your breath to listen for the barking of the dogs.

I've seen some hunters abuse the sport by allowing cruelty to the prey. That's never been my style. As an animal control officer and animal lover essentially engaged in pest control, it's important to kill as quickly and humanely as possible. Hunting is certainly cleaner, and more humane than the poison drops that leave animals in agony, for hours or days.

No two hunts are ever the same. Pig hunters, love telling their stories, over and over again, and love hearing the adventures of others.

A friend once said to me "Who wants to hear the dull truth when they can hear an exciting lie"? I disagree with this. Pig Hunting is full of anticipation, adventure and excitement. While not every trip is eventful, we seldom missed getting something and the stories I have told in this book are completely factual. Everything is to the best of my recall. I hope readers enjoy my tales as much as I have had pleasure recording them.

CHAPTER I

Beginnings

WHEN I WAS ABOUT SEVENTEEN, I was taken pig hunting for the very first time. My cousin by marriage, Dick Moore, whom I had lived with as a child at Mount Pleasant, Christchurch, took me pig hunting at Waiau for a weekend. At the time I wasn't overly impressed, as it seemed to me that we walked for miles, and the only pig we saw was disappearing over the horizon, not allowing us to have a shot at it, and so after a full day's hard exercise we returned to the hut empty handed.

Next morning we received help from some shepherds who were there with their dogs. We walked down the road not far from the house, climbed over a pig-proof fence and almost immediately got on to a mob of pigs. To my delight we ended up with five of them, and I was impressed by the difference it made by using dogs.

It wasn't until I met my friend Daniel Robin about eighteen months later that I became seriously interested in the sport. I had met Daniel through a mutual interest in motor cycles. Daniel was slightly built but tough, capable, confident and easy going. He was a very good organiser and nothing was a problem to him. "She'll be right," he often said, when sometimes it wasn't, but he never panicked about anything, and had millions of friends.

One of our first hunting trips was to Havelock in the Nelson district. We were taken out by a local called Ginger Schultz. Ginger had pig dogs and there were plenty of pigs in the immediate vicinity, and goats too, so we went for a hunt in some mature native bush, and the dogs got a big sow. It was all very exciting, the sound of barking hounds echoing through the trees; the scream of a big angry sow when they grabbed it, and the excitement of the chase, running with your heart in your mouth. I was hooked, and that was it; the beginning of my pig hunting days.

Dan was already hooked, and decided he would make an offer for one of Ginger's dogs. He offered him fifty pounds for a dog named Mate. It was a fortune in those days, but the owner was reluctant to accept the money because he said the dog wasn't worth that much.

"Why did you offer him that?" I asked Dan.

"Well, he was the first dog to bark!" he replied.

It wasn't until we took him out in open country that we found what he was doing. The dog was chasing the pigs away! He wouldn't bark at them unless they were a hundred yards ahead, and was the biggest coward I had ever seen.

This was about the time we started going to Shand's, Glen Wye and numerous other places on a regular basis. The fitter we got the keener we got and the keener we got the fitter we got, and we were always looking for new areas to hunt.

Unless you have contacts, relatives with farms or are born on a farm it could be very hard to get anywhere worthwhile to hunt, especially when the game-buyers were operating, buying pork and venison, which was considered to be in some instances the farmworkers' perk.

Diesel Dan (Daniel's nickname) and I decided we would take a day off work, and pay a visit to as many North Canterbury farms as we could fit in during the day, reasoning that it's too easy to say "no" over the telephone. We figured the owner or manager would be bound to like us if they actually met us and would say yes!

We initially avoided some places like the plague. Glen Wye was one, as the manager, Bill Gray had a fearsome reputation for dealing with poachers. Supposedly he had dug a trench with his bulldozer around a car he found on his land, and another story was that he once set fire to some scrub where a car had been hidden. I can't vouch for the truth of these stories, and they may have just been started to discourage poachers. But my cousin who knew Bill Gray swore that these things were true.

We set out and visited several properties we knew had pigs, but the farmers wouldn't give their permission, so at first we couldn't find anywhere new to hunt. Luckily we had a couple of good farms already, but you can't hunt the same properties all the time and it is nice to explore new country. We were always on the lookout for prospective locations to go to.

One weekend we were on our way home from Murchison with a trailer-load of pigs. It was getting dark and we were low on fuel, and approaching Glen Wye Station, where there was a game-buyers' depot. Bill Gray answered our knock at the door of his house, and he wasn't very keen on selling us any fuel until he discovered our trailer-load of pigs. We then reached a compromise. We sell him half our pigs and he would sell us enough fuel to enable us to get home. When it came time to put a surname on the game-buyer docket, and I told him "Broadhurst" his whole demeanour changed. Bill asked if I was related to Charlie, which I was, and he told us we could go hunting right then and there, if we wanted to. Thereafter not once was I refused permission to hunt on his property. (It's not what you know, it's who you know.) As a matter of fact, Bill even took us out in his big 4WD International flat-decked truck.

He told us about a huge boar they had nicknamed Mini Minor, that would come down and steal bones from around the dog-kennels, and another boar they called Morris 1100 which was even bigger. We later killed quite a number of boars on Bill's property, but we are not sure if the two boars he mentioned were amongst the tally.

One day on his farm the dogs chased a big sow from up in the bush above us and grabbed it beside the truck. Bill was most impressed. "Charlie's dogs would never have delivered a pig right to your truck like that," he said.

I didn't say anything, but I had climbed nearly to the top of the hill myself, and it was merely a fluke that the pig had been stopped where it had. While Bill had been parked he used his binoculars to look down to Boyle Point where he had noticed some activity going on. A couple of large high-sided trucks were parked there and men walking about, also the ground appeared to be coloured red. As we watched a light plane came in and landed on the main road, so Bill decided we should go down and have a look to see what was going on. We drove down and found the ground looked red because it was covered in deer carcasses that were being dropped there by helicopters to be loaded into the large high-sided trucks for delivery to the Christchurch game-processing factory. The light plane had been used as a spotter for mobs of deer and worked in conjunction with the helicopters.

If my memory serves me correctly, we were told that around two hundred and fifty deer had been killed that day, and they expected to get a total of six hundred if the weather stayed fine for the next couple of days.

After having been invited to hunt on Glen Wye Station I was keen to get up there as soon as possible, so was soon on the phone to arrange a hunt for the next Saturday. Bill described the area he wanted us to go to, and my hunting companion was to be Diesel Dan. The week before, the weather had not been good and by the weekend the Lewis Pass was covered in snow and the forecast was for more of the same, so Dan pulled out. I put the dogs into the boot of the Morris 1000, grabbed my old army coat and .303, and thought I would just go myself until I got a pig. All right for one to say, but when I left the road at Manuka Stream, both the dogs and I found the going tough, with no tracks visible, and hidden obstacles underfoot to catch you out.

At one stage, after pushing my way through a patch of head high manukas, I couldn't work out why I had rocks in my pockets. The old world war two army coats have decent flaps covering the pockets, but obviously not enough to keep the snow out, which got in and froze solid.

Anyway, we got a pig of about forty pounds, satisfying both the dogs and myself. No other game was sighted and it was too cold to be enjoyable.

A few weeks later I returned to the area, this time with Diesel Dan who decided he would like to shoot a deer while I would take the dogs and get a pig. Dan went up Calf Stream while I took the dogs up Gorge Stream.

The hills in the area are fairly steep, and after a couple of hours up on the hill without getting on to anything I went and crossed to the other side which will always look better no matter which side you are on. I hadn't been there long before the dogs were bailing a stroppy blue pig, which towered above them and was giving them a hard time. It wasn't until I had killed it and went to gut it I found it was a large sow. I had no string, so tried tying its legs with supplejack, but they kept coming undone, so I cut a slit in each belly flap to put my arms through. Although tight, it was ok. I then made the mistake of getting myself into the creek, which was not exactly smooth as it had large rocks with numerous bends and waterfalls.

I hadn't gone far when I was stopped by a log jam, followed by a waterfall at a sharp bend where I was forced to scramble up nearly vertically using tree roots and young trees as hand-holds until I was on a ridge overlooking a large pool into which I threw the pig, and clambered down after it.

It was wintertime, and a pig full of water is not a pleasant thing to put on one's back. I ended up soaked to the skin and freezing cold by the time I got to the main road bridge, which is about twenty-five feet above the creek. I considered climbing up to the road with the pig on my back, but had second thoughts after giving it a try for about ten feet. I realised that if I slipped I could be killed or injured, so leaving the pig on the stream bed I climbed up to the road. I stood there thinking about my next move when a passing motorist in a truck pulled over and I recognised him as Alan Orchard, one of our hunting friends. Luckily for me he was returning from the west coast at just the right time as I had only just got up onto the road, and he had a long rope which we attached one end to the pig while I pushed from below, Alan pulled. The one hundred and sixty pound sow was brought up to the road without any drama.

I had almost forgotten about Diesel Dan when a cold dishevelled figure appeared and asked for help to get the deer out he had shot. "It's just off the road, not far," he said. Alan was wearing his good shoes and trousers. We all walked for twenty minutes before we came to the stag, which was in a steep-sided creek at the bottom of a waterfall. Prior to arriving we had waded through a couple of hundred metres of knee-deep swamp, which didn't do much for Alan's "best dressed" reputation and would have definitely ruined his dancing shoes. By the time we reached the deer it was dark, we had no torches and we faced a long drag back to the car. By this time I believe Alan was having second thoughts about having stopped in the first place.

Eventually with much heaving and sweating, even though the

night was cold, we got the deer back to the car and took our animals to the game-buyer depot at Glen Wye, where Bill Gray weighed the blue sow in at one hundred and sixty pounds and was most impressed by the size of the pig's front feet, which we all agreed were the biggest feet that any of us had ever seen. As a matter of fact, after Bill Gray bought the pig from us, he cut one front foot off, and insisted I keep it for a souvenir. I had it at home for many years preserved in the largest-sized Agee preserving jar. The foot filled the jar completely, and was preserved in methylated spirits.

BRASS MONKEY WEATHER!

Three a.m. and I had just shot bolt upright to a sitting position in bed, disturbing my wife, from her sleep. "You're going to hurt yourself one of these days doing that," she said.

I didn't need an alarm clock: I could wake automatically at any time I chose if a pig hunting trip was involved. Down to the kitchen, a large glass of milk, two or three raw eggs, a quick stir and down the hatch. That's breakfast over with. Some food for the day had been prepared the night before along with all the necessary gear. The trailer was already hooked up to the car ready to receive the dogs. Soon I was on my way to pick up Diesel Dan who lived close by and also his younger brother Malcolm who had worked for the New Zealand Forest Service as a deer culler. Even in Christchurch there was a frost, but nothing compared with what we encountered when we arrived at Boyle Point in the Lewis Pass just before daybreak an hour and a half later.

Clad in bush shirts and shorts, it was freezing. The hundred metre walk from the car to the river was painful as we crunched our way through waist-high ice-covered matagouri, to the edge of a freezing snow-fed river. The dogs plunged in and started swimming for the

Author Warwick Broadhurst with "another good boar".

far side, with Dan and me in pursuit. It was so cold our legs would hardly work and ached like toothache, but Dan and I arrived on the far bank just as the dogs caught a sixty pound sow. As the initial excitement subsided we suddenly realised we hadn't seen Malcolm since we crossed the river. We found him sitting on a large rock in the middle of the river. Half way across, he felt he needed a rest, and seeing the dark outline of a large rock conveniently placed slightly downstream he had headed for it, however he had forgotten the top side would be scoured out from the action of the fast flowing water, and just as he had thought he was safe he had taken a swim, and was not happy at all.

Having never smoked I found it hard to be sympathetic to a smoker just because he had gotten his baccy and matches wet, but for Malcolm it was an absolute calamity. Luckily as the sun came

Grassington – the heaviest pig I've ever carried – 280lbs.

TOP: Me with the pig (186 lbs), and Daniel Robin.
BOTTOM: Me in the snow at Lewis Pass (Glyn Wye).

up and shone into the river terraces we all started to warm up a bit. The dogs showed a bit of interest on a ferny face nearby, and then Dan spotted the rear end of a large black boar protruding from it. As the dogs weren't near it was decided Dan would shoot, but after one shot the boar bolted straight down off the side of the hill with all the dogs in hot pursuit.

The dogs caught the boar and held it. We quickly killed the pig. He weighed one hundred and eighty-six pounds gutted, but being young and silly and with a little help from my friends I put the pig on my back before it was gutted to take some photographs. We sold the pigs on the way home and I am not sure if Malcolm has forgiven me for driving past the shop at Culverden where he was looking forward to replenishing his tobacco and matches, but I drove straight through. He was nearly in tears and wailed at me, "You don't know what it is like!" He was right, I didn't know what it was like, nor had any desire to find out and thankfully I never started.

Me, Ginger Shultz and Malcom Robin at Havelock.

TOP: Above the main road, Havelock. Note the dog Saki in the very thick undergrowth, which was difficult to negotiate. BOTTOM: A couple of pigs in the Lewis Pass. With Alan Orchard's Austin Princess.

TOP: At Lewis Pass.
BOTTOM: Jack Barker at Lewis Pass.

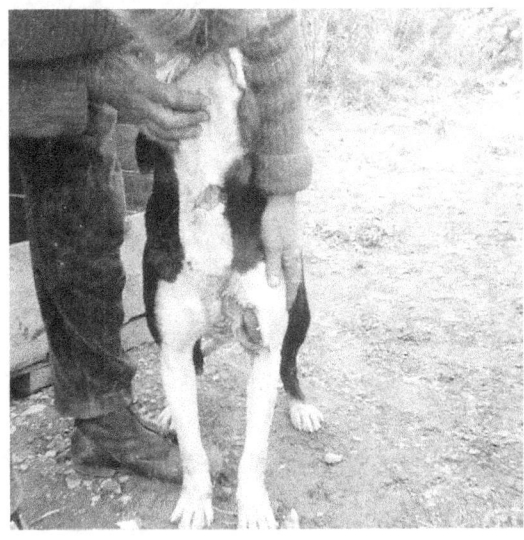

TOP: Me with a 160lb boar at Lewis Pass.
BOTTOM: Jack's dog Sam, injured by boar.

Me, and the 160 pounder, at Lewis Pass.

CHAPTER 2

The Cora Lynn Ripper

MY FRIEND DES CAMPBELL HAD arranged a trip for us to Cora Lynn in the Arthur's Pass area. Des was a ruggedly built no nonsense sort of character who always had very good dogs which he exercised twice daily in a paddock behind his house. Des suffered badly from an accident he had on his motorbike and had pins and plates in his legs. He walked with a limp, but this never stopped him or dampened his enthusiasm.

Cora Lynn is a rugged place, hot in the summer and very cold in the winter. Steep shaly hills covered in briar, matagouri, lawyer (sometimes known as 'wait-a-while' because of its grabbing hold of you properties!) and tussock. Fingers of scrubby manuka and pockets of native bush complete the scene.

After an early start we left our home town of Christchurch with a trailer full of dogs and high hopes for a successful day's hunting, as Graeme the property manager had told Des that his sheep dogs had several times bailed what he assumed to be a boar. The unusual thing was that this animal always retreated to the thickest available cover, fought the dogs off, then before any of them realised what had happened, he tip-toed out the back door and with a head start outran the dogs. Anyway, that is what we assumed was happening because no-one we knew had actually seen the pig.

The two and a half-hour trip was uneventful and we arrived at the farm just before daybreak to find Graeme up and the billy boiled. After a quick cuppa and a brief discussion on the plan of attack we headed for the area where Graeme had noticed fresh pig rooting which had been returned to night after night until it looked like a war-zone. As first light approached we left the house to walk the short distance to where the boar had been coming out.

We went across a stony creek-bed, up through some black birch, and around the foot of the steep hill. The frost was a good one and the ground frozen solid. I noticed my finder, Ricky, a liver and white staghound springer spaniel-cross, showing some interest on the steep frozen tussock face above us so after a quick discussion I followed the direction my dog had taken while Des and Graeme kept below us.

I found the frozen ground very slippery, so when Ricky started barking in the next gully my progress was a bit slower than normal. Unable to travel very fast, I couldn't catch up with the pig and the dog. They were at least one gully ahead. Finally I came to a point where I could overlook a scrub-covered shingle fan. Down below I saw Ricky looking into a thick clump of scrub, barking all the while.

As I watched, the barking tapered off and the dog put his nose down and took off diagonally across the flat country heading towards the main highway a few hundred metres away. I could see well ahead of the dog but at no time saw the pig.

That was our first encounter with the boar we later came to call the Cora Lynn Ripper.

After a further unsuccessful trip in which we walked all day covering a lot of hard country, I arrived back at our vehicle just on dusk. The car was parked in a paddock fifty metres off the main road on the edge of a riverbed. I put my dogs in the trailer and waited for Des to arrive. I could see him making his way back through the scrub and he was within shouting distance when suddenly there was a short burst of barking and Des yelled to let the dogs out of the trailer. The pig got away again. Apparently what had happened was that Brownie, Des's old bull mastiff boxer, had come across the pig in a thick patch of scrub right in front of Des. The dog gave a couple of barks and grabbed an ear but was promptly thrown off. The pig did his normal Houdini act and escaped again without being seen. After this, getting that pig became an obsession with Des and he started going back and staying overnight with Graeme and his family. The beauty of this is that he got to have an evening as well as a morning hunt.

On one of these hunts Ricky had a boar bailed high on a rocky face for over an hour, but Des said that every time he climbed to a certain point he would lose the sound and thought the pig had gone. Every time he went back down the hill the barking was clear again. So up the hill once more and keep going until he found where they were. Unfortunately the old dog Brownie rushed in and tried to hold the pig, which just threw him off and then bolted. Des said that at the time he was very close but never saw the pig. This pig was proving to be very elusive. We considered our dogs to be reasonably good except for poor old Brownie who had been a good dog in his day but was well past his prime. Shortly after that Brownie was found a new home.

By this stage we had been after this pig for months and still hadn't seen it. We discussed whether it might have been a barrow which wasn't leaving as strong a scent as one left by a boar. Boars gave a pungent sweet aniseed smell. The other thing that came to mind was that maybe the dogs had been beaten so many times by this pig they became a little half-hearted in their pursuit. It was with this thought in mind that I approached another very close pig hunting mate and asked for a loan of his two dogs.

My friend John Roberts had an old foxy-cross named Trev, an excellent finder and bailer even though he must have been at least a hundred years old in human terms. The second dog, Ned, was a brindle bulldog-cross which I had bred myself and sold to John as a pup. My old bulldog bitch Jean had produced many good pig dogs – all of them naturals and John's dog was no exception. The only arguments we had ever had were over whose dog was the pick of the litter!

The day we took Ned and Trev with us, a nor-wester was in the air. Nor-westers usually start with a calm period in the early morning before the day breaks, followed by strong gusty winds as the sun rises, and this day was to be no exception. Although we tried our best to keep the dogs in sight at all times the inevitable happened and Ned and Trev soon disappeared without us and we were unable to tell which direction they had taken.

Des and I searched high and low sometimes catching a faint bark on the wind but not able to pinpoint the location. We were standing on a scrubby face about a hundred metres apart with a small gully between us, and above us about one hundred metres up was native bush. I was facing Des when suddenly out of the corner of my eye I noticed a pig hurtling down towards him. Maybe it detected Des somehow, as moments before it reached him it veered into the gully and passed between us.

Des let out a couple of shots from his 30/30 carbine but the pig was gone quickly and the dogs didn't seem to be able to pick up the scent. The two dogs, Ned and Trev, came back looking worn out and it was obvious that they had held on until they couldn't hold on any longer.

That was our first look at the Cora Lynn Ripper. He was quite a distinctive boar – black with a ginger tint. Not terribly big but good even tusks and very fit. Once again he ran down from the hill and headed toward the main road disappearing from sight on the flattish country between, while the dogs showed little or no interest in tracking him, it was almost as if there had never been a pig there at all.

We didn't go back to the property for a few months, and when we did Des dropped me and my two dogs Ricky and Spook (who was the progeny of the old dog Jean and the neighbour's collie Labrador-cross) at the high point on the road where it passes above a bluff enabling me to get a bit of a start up the steep hillside.

Des, in the meantime, was going to hunt the front country about a mile ahead of me. The idea was that I was to hunt the sunny faces and the terraces, all the time working my way back to the car which was to be parked off the side of the road near some willows.

The dogs worked well together. Ricky, always with his nose to the ground, had a tireless gait and could go for days without giving up. Being liver and white in colour he was a very good dog to spot, especially in poor light and in tussock country. Spook wind-scented and was always on the move, although usually not far from his mate.

On this day I made my way uphill, pausing now and again to listen for the dogs. They had been gone about twenty minutes and I was standing on the hill looking back into a terrace I had just climbed. The hillside was scrub covered with exposed patches of clay while about two hundred yards further on, a bush gully undulated into the terrace face.

Suddenly the dogs appeared on the terrace below.

Spook came up to greet me before returning to his mate who was on the trail of something, and headed flat out toward the bush gully. I stood watching as they disappeared out of sight.

A few seconds later loud barking erupted followed by continuous squealing. They had a pig!

I kept on the same level until I entered the bush, then, drawing my bayonet, I ran directly downhill toward the dogs that had a good-sized black pig by an ear each. Suddenly I realised there was no more bush behind the dogs – just daylight. The rear end of the pig appeared to slip off the edge. I screamed at the dogs to let go. Surprisingly they did, as it is not in their nature to release a pig once they have one – they must have detected the sheer terror in my voice.

There was a rattle of stones, a brief pause and a short squeal as the pig ricocheted off the cliff face. I felt sick. I did not know the drop was there and I had nearly lost my two mates. I pulled them close and hugged them both.

I tried to find the pig. It took about thirty minutes to find a way around and get to the bottom of the drop. Looking up, I estimated the height to be around three hundred feet. Pieces of the cliff – as big as houses – had fallen off at some time in the past and then large trees had grown out of the tops of them. I never did find the pig; it could have landed in a tree top or one of the crevasses formed by the massive chunks that had come down.

After working my way back to the vehicle, a cool breeze sprang up followed by a few spots of rain. As I didn't know where Des had hidden the key I found a sheltered spot and lay in the tussock to keep warm. I was there for twenty minutes and it started to spit with rain, but by that time I had discovered the car keys underneath the rock on which I had been resting.

Meanwhile the dogs had gone for a drink in a pool below the nearby willows, so when they returned I put them in the trailer. Shortly after that they started vomiting. They had obviously eaten some poison. They bought up so much fluid and mucus I took the dogs out and stood the tailer up on end to drain it.

It was getting late in the day when Des returned and we swapped stories of the day's events. Des had stopped his van within sight of boar sign that was fresh that morning and reckoned that if we had been together we would have had a pig. I had a look through Des's binoculars and could plainly see along the bottom of the hill patches of thistles rooted up so I decided to walk back to the farm that was a mile away while Des drove the van.

I took Girl with me this time – a littermate to my dog Spook and a very good hunter. Starting out, the pig sign I ran across was plentiful and the dogs had gained a bit of new life after a rest, but by the time we were halfway back to the homestead, the sign had petered out and I resigned myself to having had a bad day.

Suddenly close by there was a couple of barks and a snort, then heavy breathing. The dogs had a boar in his bed. It was impossible to get into them. I could smell the pungent sweet smell of the pig – it was only a couple of feet below, but I couldn't get through. I ran to one end of the thicket and tried to force my way through but it was impossible.

Next minute the pig broke, straight downhill – still inside the thick scrub.

I stood for a few seconds listening, and next thing my black dog

Spook came back to me. This was most unusual, but when I thought about it later I realised he had just been very sick after drinking the water by the willows and was probably weakened by it all. I walked down through the scrub until I came to a fence behind which was a green paddock with black cattle in it. By this time it was nearly dusk and I noticed the cattle at the far ends of the paddock run to one corner, and stop and look back. I followed the direction of their gaze and at the same time heard Girl and Ricky bailing. There on the burnt manuka face stood a black boar. It was the Cora Lynn Ripper, hackles up and grinding his tusks. Without another thought I jumped the fence, ran straight across the paddock, leapt over the far fence, across a dry creek bed, up a metre high shingle bank with my bayonet in my hand while Ricky and Girl wouldn't go within thirty feet of the boar. I was wishing I had a gun, but by then I had forgotten about Spook.

All of a sudden he popped up bedside me, took one look at the boar and headed flat out up the hill at him. We arrived at almost the same time. Spook grabbed the right ear and I plunged the bayonet through his left side into the pig's heart without laying a hand on him.

There is an old rule in pig hunting that you never approach a pig from below when it is bailed especially when it has a clear view of you but sometimes any fear of personal injury is overcome by the desire to protect your dogs which after all would do the same for you every time.

I realised later that the paddock I had cut across had an electric fence around it and this is why I had beaten the dog as he had taken the longer route – the same route taken by the other dogs and the boar.

By the time the boar was gutted it was dark. I was within a couple of hundred metres of the main road, so I waited until a vehicle with lights passed by and then I would quickly look where to go and drag the pig, then wait for the next set of lights to help me see where

I was going and repeat the process until I was back on the road.

I left the pig on the side of the road, then went back to the house saying nothing to my companions straight away. Later I said "Oh, by the way, I got that boar you have been after," and they looked at me with disbelief, thinking I was having them on, till I pointed out the blood on my hands. We brought the pig back to Christchurch and sold him the next day.

It was a bit sad to see the end of such a worthy foe, but no doubt he would have left progeny to carry on his bloodlines. He was a ripper of a pig, he lead us a merry dance. He weighed in at one hundred and thirty-seven pounds dressed (not a big pig) but had a good even jaw, and aptly deserved his given name "The Cora Lynn Ripper".

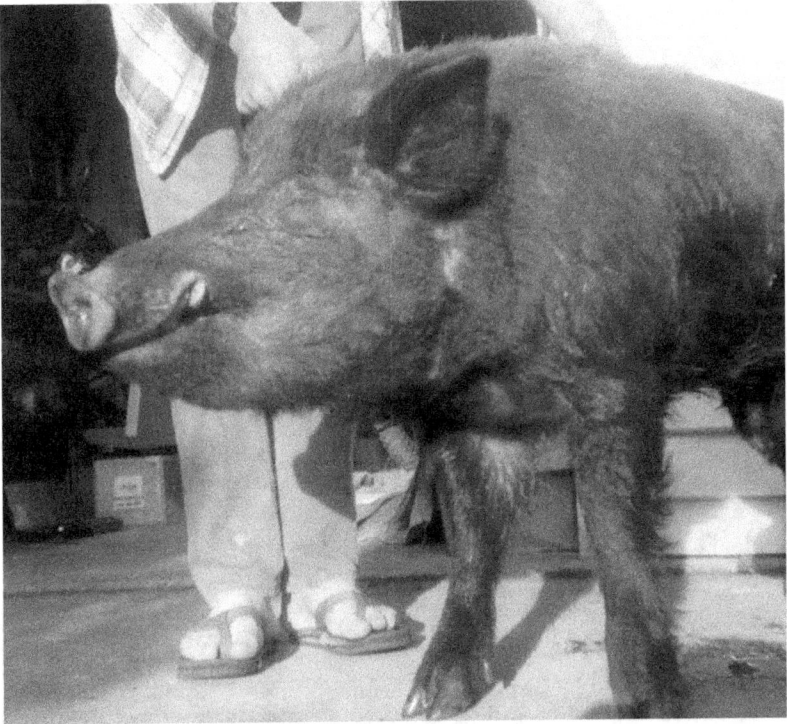

The Cora Lynn Ripper – 137lbs.

TOP: The Cora Lynn Ripper.
BOTTOM: Damage caused by pig rooting at Lewis Pass.

TOP: Leadervale, Waiau 140 lb boar. Dave and me.
BOTTOM: Bob Brett's Boar, Flock Hill 150 lbs.

190lb Boar.

CHAPTER 3

Murchison Pigs

THE DAY DAWNED GREY, WITH the early morning mists hanging low and obscuring the mountaintops. Des and I had returned to the hut at Murchison the night before for a weekend of hunting. The drive from Christchurch had been uneventful except that when we had stopped at Murchison for the evening we found that one of the dog-trailer doors had come open and one of Des's dogs was no longer with us having departed somewhere between Springs Junction and Murchison, but where exactly was anybody's guess. There wasn't much we could do other than to phone a few of the farmers along the way and ask them to keep an eye out for the dog, and try not to let the bad start ruin our weekend.

With this still on our minds we headed off up the River Flats wondering what excitement the day would bring. About half a mile into our journey we were dismayed to hear the sound of a helicopter approaching from behind, flying below the cloud ceiling that was only a few hundred feet above ground level. The pilot's ears should have been burning as we made a few uncomplimentary remarks about their hunting methods as we watched the machine disappearing ahead of us with its accompanying cacophony of noise warning any game that humans were on the hunt.

With our enthusiasm slightly dampened we rounded a bend in the river where the land opened out to a large grassy flat. It was here that the dogs became very keen and were soon racing in circles looking for the animal that had obviously been out during the night.

Suddenly Des said, "Look at that!" and pointed at a steep ferny face a couple of hundred metres away. High on the hill a large black boar was racing for its life. Below him my staghound springer spaniel-cross had his nose down and was on the scent with the rest of the dogs strung out behind him. I ran as quickly as I could, across the flat, up the steep track through the fern, trying to avoid tripping on the hidden rocks and debris from trees that had once grown there but had long been removed when the land was cleared for farming. Before I was halfway to them I could hear the dogs bailing just over the top of a small rise before the hill rose steeply again. As I pushed through the fern I came face to face with a large black boar, hackles up, and grinding his tusks. At that time the dogs we had were either pups or bailing dogs, but not good hard reliable holders, so they were facing the boar from a distance of about six feet, keeping his attention. The only firearm was back down on the flat with Des and I knew he wouldn't be coming to us, but would be waiting patiently for our return.

Bayonet in hand, and keeping an eye on the pig, I climbed over a half-covered log, about a metre tall, and sidled around until I was behind the boar. Jumping over the log I grabbed the boar by the tail and leaned forward to stick him through the brisket, but as soon as I struck I knew I had missed the vital spot. This pig was big, tall and long. The boar moved forward dragging me with him through the fern, off the small level area we were on, and over the side of the hill, until we cartwheeled end over end down a steep face together.

My first fear was that I might end up underneath one very angry tusker, or draped over the sharp end. I was surprised to find on stopping, that we were on another small ledge. I still had the boar by the tail, and hadn't dropped my knife from my right hand.

Quickly I leaned forward, further this time, and struck the heart. The boar moved forward again, once more causing us to cartwheel down the hill. I let the pig's tail go and ended up upside down in a large lawyer bush, while the pig continued to roll down-hill towards Des, who was busy loading up his 30/30 thinking he was about to be attacked.

Now all this exercise and excitement had taken its toll on me and I was lying upside down in a lawyer bush gasping for breath, while Des was trying to have a long distance conversation with me. "Haven't you stuck it yet?" and, "Are you hurt?" With great difficulty I managed to gasp out, "It's dead! I can't breathe". A minute or two later I had recovered sufficiently to extract myself from the prickles and follow the crushed undergrowth where the boar lay dead. Once gutted, the legs were tied to form a pack, and the pig was rolled on to my back and I stood up. The ground underfoot was swampy and very soft, and after standing for a few seconds in the one spot, I found I couldn't lift my legs out of the mud, so it was off with the pig and the carcass cut in half just below the rib cage. Now, the front half would have to be one of the most uncomfortable and difficult objects a hunter could carry, and as usual I had drawn the short straw and got the front to carry the kilometre back to the closest point we could get the car to. When the two halves were weighed they totaled two hundred and twenty-eight pounds (104 kg).

Des's lost dog was returned to him a week later after an ad in the paper was answered by a farmer, although not before the farmer had to be convinced by Des that he was not a poacher, and the dog really had fallen off the trailer. All's well that ends well.

Every trip to Murchison was an adventure and pigs were plentiful. Why we started out so early one trip I will never know. It was three a.m. Dan Robin, Keith Churcher, Sam Saunders and I were half way between Springs Junction and Murchison in my 1956 Ford Customline. The road in those days was shingle and had numerous bends. We were all half asleep when suddenly in the middle of the road appeared a huge stag with a really good head. That woke the boys up in a hurry, but we were unprepared. Keith grabbed a rifle from the back seat, nearly putting a hole through the windscreen with the barrel. In a flash the stag ran up a bank, jumped a fence and was gone leaving us now wide awake but rueing the fact that were not better prepared.

We were on the way to Murchison to have a weekend at a farm owned by friends David and Zita. They lived there with their seven children at the end of a remote valley. Every week they and their children filled their 1947 Chevrolet to capacity and then some for their trip into town for church on Sundays. They always made us feel welcome and we drank a lot of their tea, and spent a lot of time yakking about nothing in particular but everything in general from hunting to politics. Around the vicinity of the house would be pigs, pups and bare-footed kids along with chooks. Pigs were free to roam, so could become an embarrassment if the dogs started getting them. Obviously our dogs were kept in the dog-trailer or the boot of the car when we were near the house.

When we first went to the farm, there were the remnants of an old sawmill with a small room at one end made from planks, and covered in tarpaper or malthoid to keep the constant rain out. Just large enough to sleep four on the floor, it at least kept us dry. This accommodation was about eight hundred metres further in from the house and saved us from having to erect tents. The pigs were mainly black and white, black and tan, or the odd black one. Nowadays the coloured pigs have become less common and there are more grey, black, cream or solid colours. Once, while returning to our hut from a morning hunt we got a hell of a surprise when one of the dogs started to bark at the hut door as we approached it. Luckily we were able to quickly grab the dogs and tie them up to find a mob of pigs inside eating our food and turning our sleeping bags over with their snotty noses. I'd had a roasted fore-quarter of mutton in a biscuit tin. That was gone, along with anything else that wasn't in tins. We kicked them out and never saw them again. We told David, but he wasn't very concerned, these were his "tame" wild pigs he had forgotten to tell us to watch out for.

Apparently the wild pigs at Murchison are descended from tame ones that had escaped after the big earthquake of the early 1930s when David, the owner of the farm, which we regularly hunted, was a boy at primary school. He told me that during the earthquake the teacher shepherded the kids out on to the play-ground, which was rising and falling like the ocean, then on his way home up the valley the terrain was unrecognisable due to the numerous slips.

The dogs had bailed up one old boar on a steep narrow muddy track in the bush but they were unable to get at it, and the only person with a firearm was Keith, who was stuck on a bluff on the bush above, but luckily could see through the trees and saw the pig. So after calling the dogs off, Keith shot it. We probably did him a favour as when we went to gut him we found he was covered in cysts and he had shotgun pellets throughout his hide. Anyway he was rotten, but we were still going to bring him out for a trophy, and carried him for quite a while until as we were sidling around a steep area just above the river, a slip and he was in the water and gone. All that effort wasted, but no real loss.

On the Saturday nights, we would either stay up talking half the night, or go into Murchison for a beer or two, then come back to share some with the family. Once while on my own I was following what remained of an old logging track through thick bush. The track wound in and out and I was fairly certain the dogs were on to something below me as that was where they were last seen heading. Bee had stayed back with me, and after rounding a sharp bend he put his nose down and headed straight uphill at a fast pace with me in pursuit. There was no noise, not a bark, nothing. After a couple of hundred metres we came to a ridge and sure enough down the other side the dogs had a nice black boar. If I had not had Bee with me, I most likely would not have found them and they could have come back worn out or worse, injured.

The boar was facing downhill on a steep muddy track that was very hard to keep your footing on, and as I went to stick him I kept sliding and nearly overtook the lot of them. I started at the back of the boar and kept sliding past them, but luckily managed to kill the pig before I ended up in front. Incredibly I only had to drag the carcass downhill to the edge of a track where I could get to my vehicle, and then roll him straight from the bank to the tailgate. The pig was one hundred and eighty pounds, and no carrying was necessary!

While talking to my friend David, the farmer at Murchison, he was concerned that pigs had been eating his lambs and suggested that we go out in the middle of the night hunting for the pig or pigs causing the problems. We didn't have much in the way of torches, and most of David's family came with us. We trudged up the muddy track on the way up to the area where the sheep and lambs were, a five kilometre walk in the dark. We were a bit like *Dad's Army*, a motley crew of adults and children dressed in an assortment of warm clothing, gumboots, parkas and lambies, anything to keep ourselves warm and dry.

I hate hunting in the dark unless it is spotlighting and we didn't have anything even faintly resembling a spotlight. My dogs were Carl, Bee and Ricky, and there was no moon, which made it more difficult. The track was exceptionally muddy. I didn't want the dogs to go running off on their own, and was forever having to call them in. Eventually after walking through five kilometres of bush we arrived in an open area where the sheep were. We could hear the ewes baaing and there were little bleats and lambs calling for their mothers all over the fern-covered hill.

I had to trust my dogs when they went in amongst the stock. It was pitch black, and I held my breath as I listened while they hunted on the hill above us, so it was with great relief I finally heard a bark followed by continuous squealing. The dogs had a good sow. We had spoken about pigs eating lambs before, and we agreed that pigs don't have to be very big to kill and eat lambs, and they learn from one another very quickly. They eat the afterbirth, and get a taste for the little lambs while they still smell of blood so the lambs don't have a chance. I was relieved to get at least one because if I had to follow my dogs too far we would have had no battery power left in our torches which were almost flat by this time and I would never have kept up with them in the dark. It was very stressful. I thought, "What am I doing here?" It was a catch-twenty-two situation really, because most farmers don't want dogs running around amongst newborn lambs because they can become mis-mothered, but of course neither do they want them eaten by pigs, so neither of us could win.

When David was out on the hill one day a sheepdog bailed a boar. Now the boar wasn't very concerned about the dog and made no effort to run, but the dog kept up a steady bark and David was unarmed, and because the pig made no effort to get away, he tied the dog up near it and headed off home to get his rifle. It took the best part of half an hour before he returned and the position had been reversed: the pig was giving the dog a hard time and the poor dog couldn't get away. David got there just in time to save his dog, which by this time had had enough of being harassed, and he shot the pig.

The road through the Lewis Pass to the coast from Christchurch used to be a winding shingle one. I was travelling through it late one night about 1955 with a friend, George Stewart, and driving my 1935 Ford V8 which on the shingle and pot-holed road was quite noisy due to the car having old-fashioned brake rods which rattled with the ruts and pot-holes in the road. The lights of the old car were very poor, like candles, being only a six-volt system and it was difficult to see. We were driving along not far above the Waiau River, when suddenly we heard a loud high-pitched pulsating noise, which sounded similar to today's burglar alarms, woooooo-wooooo! I first thought something had gone wrong with the car. I pulled over, and wound down the driver's window, and listened. The sound was exceptionally loud, all-around all encompassing, and it sounded like it was just above the car. I couldn't identify the source of the noise. The hair stood up on the back of my neck!

I quickly wound the window up and drove as fast as I could, until a few kilometres down the road it just suddenly stopped as quickly as it had started, and I have never heard a sound quite like that since. There was no electricity through the Lewis Pass in those days, so it wasn't that. I wondered if the sound had something to do with some type of thermal activity, as there are hot springs throughout the area, but I never found an explanation for that puzzling and quite frightening incident.

The hunting camp at Murchison.

TOP: Alan Orchard, Sam Saunders and me.
BOTTOM: Hut scene.

MURCHISON PIGS

TOP: Daniel and Sam.
BOTTOM: The three wheeled Gnat with Daniel and me at the old sawmill.

TOP: Seven pigs and a goat.
BOTTOM: This is the 228 lbs pig I rolled down the hill with.

TOP: The pig at the foot of the hill.
BOTTOM: Ricky the dog with Murchison pig.

TOP: Another day's hunt (old sawmill in the background) With Gary Smith and Sam Saunders. BOTTOM: Pat McGregor and me in steep country at Murchison (no tracks up here).

MURCHISON PIGS

TOP: Dan's Hut which replaced the old sawmill.
BOTTOM: Me with a load of pigs.

LEFT: Me and a Murchison boar RIGHT: Me and Pat McGregor.
BOTTOM: Dieter Steineg and Pat McGregor.

CHAPTER 4

Choose Your Companions Carefully

THIS GUY WAS NOT A nice person; the only reason I went hunting with him was that he was a workmate in my job. (I will call the workmate Burt to save him from any embarrassment.) I should have been warned when one day, as we sat in the open air by a beautiful bay on Banks Peninsular having lunch, a little male sparrow came up and was taking bread from my fingers and Burt said seriously, "Quick, I will get my hammer and kill it." I was shocked and I was so angry I retorted. "If you kill that sparrow I will kill you." I found out later that he was also a petty thief, not a man of good character at all.

Choose carefully who you hunt with, particularly if they are carrying a firearm, or you could very easily lose your life and end up just another hunting statistic. Our work colleague was keen to go out and had no dogs, which was a plus as we had enough at the time and had no room for more, but he did own a .303 rifle. There were four of us that day, and four dogs. Burt invited a friend of his called Dick. So there were Old Jack and I and these other two driving up to Oxford where we arrived at daybreak, a perfect morning, and a nice fine day was forecast. As we left the open paddocks and started up the hill we sidled around the edge of a nice clean open creek. We hadn't gone far when we disturbed a mob of deer. They exploded out of there with dogs in hot pursuit, so I ran up the spur, which took me fifty metres up the side to see if I could see anything. What greeted me was a stag running backwards and forwards through a burnt manuka face beneath me.

I yelled out for Burt to get up here with his rifle, as all I had was a .22. Before he had time to get there the stag appeared on the face across the valley and he was in full flight two hundred metres away, and quickly due to disappear from sight forever. In desperation I raised the .22, placed the sights about 6 feet above the stag's head and fired two quick shots. I was very surprised when the animal went straight down and didn't move, so I made a careful note of where he fell beside some scrub and big rocks, as it was too far away to see the carcass with the naked eye. My first thought was that I must have fluked a shot to the back of the head. By this time Burt had arrived huffing and puffing and very excitable. I pointed out where the deer had fallen and made him promise not to shoot unless the deer got up and made a break for it. I still could not believe the deer was going to stay down, as I made my way across the hill while Burt kept watch from the spur. I had only just arrived over there when world war three erupted and bullets were going everywhere – zzzz, splat, zzzzz, splat, zzzzzz, splat. Burt emptied his magazine in my direction though I was in the line of fire and he couldn't see me. I found the stag which was groggy, but not going anywhere, and I cut its throat. I felt it should have been Burt's throat!

He admitted later that the rock that I told him to keep an eye on appeared to move. The harder he stared the more convinced he was that it was moving, until in the end he emptied his magazine with me in line of fire. Unbelievable! The stag was one hundred

Good hunting companion Maurie Smith with Cass and Sooty at Motonau.

and fifty-six pounds on the hook, and I found I had hit him in the balls, and surprisingly that was enough to knock him down and keep him there.

The final straw with Burt came on our next trip to the same property. Burt and Dick would walk half way up along the scrubby faces which had patches of bush dotted here and there while I went to go up to the tops and walk above them while keeping a lookout below, and keeping the pair of them in sight. Eventually I decided to go down and speak to them as they were heading from the bush into a creek. Dick saw me first and tapped Burt on the shoulder and pointed to me. I was no more than three metres away as Burt with a frightened look on his face swung his rifle from the hip and pointed it directly at me. I said, "I hope there's nothing in that." His reply was, "Oh, but I didn't have my finger on the trigger though," which was not what I saw. He pointed a loaded and cocked rifle at me, and his finger was on the trigger. I wasn't going to wait until I was shot for him to learn his lesson. Burt never got another invite to go hunting with us. Choose your hunting mates carefully!

MY FRIEND DANIEL

Daniel Robin and I hunted together often, and we were a good team. He was a good guy to have with you. He was keen, fit and level-headed, and as I mentioned previously he was never ruffled about anything. Once when we arrived at Kaikoura for a hunt he went to put his boots on and found he had kicked one out of the car accidently when we stopped by the roadside for a comfort stop. Daniel managed to find a sandshoe for the other foot. He said it was alright, but reckoned he could only go one way around the hill!

One of the places we hunted at Oxford we used to call the Bald Spur, now fifty years later it is covered in thick re-growth, and is anything but bald. Any pigs that we got there we certainly earned, as it was hard country to work. Bald Spur is one of those spurs that you followed thinking you were arriving at the top, only to find the terrain continued to rise again steeply, until eventually after several rises you will come to the top, which is covered in native bush.

We knew there were a lot of deer up at Bald Spur but there was also a lot of cover, so we formed a plan where I would give Daniel a twenty minute start while he climbed to the top. On the other side there was a large rock he could sit on and observe any animals coming up through a low saddle which was frequently used by deer. Our strategy was that after 20 minutes I would bring the dogs around through the bush below the saddle, thereby hopefully driving any animals up towards Daniel. I would take my time going through the bush with my dogs, and come up below him. This was the best way we knew to get a deer when we wanted one, and we proved it worked.

Early one morning, while pig hunting, Diesel Dan and I started out in the dark and we were about half way to the top of the Bald Spur when we could tell the dogs had something just on the edge of the bush. We could hear heavy breathing and when I first looked in the darkness I could make out a light-coloured animal, and thought it was a deer, but quickly realized my mistake. It was a boar. The dogs only had it for a couple of minutes, and I quickly stuck it, and then noticed the dogs had been ripped. Saki had been ripped from under his stomach to nearly the top of his back twice. Luckily the wounds were only skin deep about an inch apart. Had they been any deeper the dog would have been disembowelled. Prince and Dinda sustained several pokes to their necks, while Hutch escaped without injury. We realized then that the dogs needed veterinary treatment immediately. My recollection is a bit vague at this point, but Daniel tells me that I took the dogs to the vet, while he dragged the pig down to the roadside and waited till I returned again in his car.

Dave (Daniel) Robin.

It was had been a very frosty winter's morning when we started out and Daniel was cold, so he looked for something to wear, and his wife Jean had left her fur coat in his car, so he had worn it up the hill. Unfortunately it became covered in blood, during the trip back to the car, so being a bit worried about Jean's reaction as the coat was special, having been made for her by her mother, he decided

Daniel Robin at Craigieburn. Boar 160 lbs.

his best plan of action would be to throw it away in the dump and deny all knowledge of it!

Sometime later Jean was driving down a road in Christchurch, and saw a girl on a push-bike wearing a coat which looked very much like her lost one, so she pulled the girl over and asked her where she had got her coat from, and said that if she didn't tell her she would take her to the police station! The poor girl became very frightened, and told her that her father had picked it up at the dump, and he found it in very dirty condition and covered in blood, so he had had it dry-cleaned. Jean did get her coat back, Daniel was in trouble as he often was, and had to buy Jean another coat as well to make up for it.

PETER ROBIN

My friend Peter Robin, younger brother of Diesel Dan, and I had planned a trip to Waiau to a friend's farm where we arrived before daybreak My friend Peter is a confirmed bachelor, though was always very popular with the ladies, good-looking, quick-witted, generous, and best of all one of the most honest persons you could ever meet. Peter was always good company and a lot of fun – one of the best companions I have ever had, and a loyal friend to this day.

Pete was an honest hard-working man, from a family of seven boys and one girl. As none of the boys were particularly tall he used to joke that his family were Snow White and the Seven Dwarfs. He was a crack shot, and used to work for the government as a deer culler. Pete is still one of my closest friends; he lives in the Marlborough Sounds, and frequently provides my wife and me with venison and blue cod, saying, "We have to look after the pensioners!"

Peter Robin and me.

We hunted together quite a lot in those early days and then we left for Australia together for a working holiday. We worked over there as roofers. Pete stayed for just six months, and I for two years. As soon as the weather became hot over there, Pete hated it, and was missing his hunting too much, so just had to come home.

The day he returned, I flew back with him for just one week. This was memorable because it was Melbourne Cup day, 1972, and a hot cloudless day, and we drove straight past Flemington, which was humming with activity. All the ladies were dressed in their finery with their fancy hats and the latest fashions, and we were worried we would be late for the plane because of the traffic congestion caused by the races. We did arrive on time, and eventually took off. As the plane rose, it did not seem to gather customary speed, and instead of pointing in the direction of NZ and given the gas, it started circling Tullamarine Airport without gathering speed.

All of a sudden a voice came over the intercom. "This is your captain speaking. We have had a slight malfunction and we are going to have to return to Tullamarine, but first we are going to go out over the sea and jettison some fuel."

We flew out over some mangrove swamps at not a great height, where we saw clouds of vapour which we presumed was fuel pouring out of the wings I said to Peter, "This is your fault, I did not want to fly home today," to which Peter replied, "I didn't want to come to Australia in the first place!"

Surrounding passengers were visibly upset and a girl behind us started crying, so we shut up – we were only making light of it. As we approached the airport we could see a line-up of fire engines and ambulances both sides of the runway. We held our breath, and we landed without incident, the firemen came up and inspected the plane from the outside, and we disembarked after being told we would probably be there for four hours, but we were in fact held up for about eight hours when they put us into another plane and we flew home without ever being told what the problem was.

Now Pete preferred to hunt without dogs and I without a rifle, so we were a good team. He had worked for the government as a deer culler and was an excellent shot with his Browning 270 semi-automatic. That day at Waiau we had a successful morning's hunt and ended up with total of eight pigs of varying sizes, four shot by Peter and four got by the dogs, but this was nothing to get excited about. The weather had turned hot and we were exhausted from our exertions and the early start of three a.m. from Christchurch. We needed to take a break and have some tucker and quench our thirst, so we retired back to the hut for a lie down.

Around midday we were sound asleep when we were both woken by a booming voice shouting out, "Get up, you lazy bastards, come and give us a hand to get the hay in." It was John, the hired help.

I should explain here that for many years my footwear of choice was the flimsiest and cheapest sand shoes imaginable. I had been out in all types of country, shaly mountain tops, floundered through snow and sat on the hills with my feet inside the dead pigs to keep my feet warm, and never had any trouble with my feet. The sandshoes were great for river crossings because they didn't hold any water, but there came a time I thought I would try some heavy boots. The boots felt quite comfortable, but were heavy and stiff and felt like blocks of concrete on my feet after what I had been used to.

That morning I realised my feet were hurting me terribly. When I looked at them they were a mess, blisters all over my feet had come up, and then broken and I couldn't put the boots back on and the only other footwear I had were a pair of jandals. They were all I could put on my feet, so Pete and I spent the rest of that day tossing hay bales and stacking them in the shed. This was not what we had gone there for but we weren't in a position to refuse because it is give and take in the country and giving us access to the country to hunt was more important to us than having to do a wee bit of work for it. We didn't complain.

Paraflex boots were something new, and I threw away the Ansons and bought a pair of soft Paraflex boots after that, which never gave me blisters and were very comfortable. After a couple of years I tried wearing my old cheap flimsy sandshoes, and I couldn't do it. The soles of my feet became sore, and I felt every rock and sharp object, so I suppose it is what you get used to. I have no doubt that if I had kept wearing those sandshoes I would have been ok.

That evening we walked out to go hunting without the dogs. To please Peter I had left the dogs behind, and he had borrowed a .303 from his brother for me to use. The cool breeze around my ankles and heels was bliss. Even though I was walking through paddocks with thistles and other prickles I felt nothing. As we walked along a ridge we looked across a small gully covered in thick manuka, and Peter spotted a sow opposite us. He said "Do you want me to shoot it now, or leave it till on the way back?" We both laughed, the pig would have been gone by then. "You had better shoot it now!" I said.

He carefully lined the pig up, pulled the trigger and the pig ran away! This was most unusual. Peter never missed anything, but I was used to his brother, who at that stage rarely hit anything, although to be fair to Diesel Dan he would later become an excellent marksman!

We continued out, the light was fading rapidly, but we had a good view of the surrounding countryside through the binoculars. There was no shortage of pigs. We could see a mob on top of a green knob, and other pigs on different parts of the property but they were too far off to get to before dark. As darkness approached we settled in for the night. The weather was clear, it had been warm during the day, so we selected a nice patch of fern, got into our sleeping bags in a standing position and jumped backwards into the fern where we had a really comfortable night's sleep, to awaken at first light to another warm day.

"Look at that!" Peter suddenly exclaimed, and there, about fifty yards below us on the same hill we were on, was a boar rooting around on the hillside. He saw us at about the same time and by the time we were able to scramble out of sleeping bags and grab our rifles it was gone, with a couple of shots helping it on its way. In one way I was disappointed because I felt that we could have had all the pigs we could carry with just the dogs the night before, and we could have been back to the hut and had a good night's sleep there.

We still had eight pigs to pick up, so before the sun was too high in the sky we went back to the farm where luckily the Gnat had been left, and we used it to pick up the pigs. But I had to come down a spur with the pigs on board and the Gnat was overloaded so I decided not to ride in it but to put the tiller around to the front position so that I could lead it without being on it if anything went wrong. We were getting along quite well and slowly coming down the spur, with the engine holding it back when I lost control, the load shifted and the Gnat went cart-wheeling down into a gully through young scrubby Manuka and ended up in a swampy area at the bottom of the hill, leaving a trail of tools, and spare chain links. The toolbox had sprung open and the pigs, which had been tied on, were distributed from the top of the trail of destruction to the bottom of the gully. We spent a considerable amount of time retrieving all the bits and pieces including the pigs and tying them on board for another go, but this time we managed not to flip it. The pigs had to be got out while they were still acceptable for the game packers to buy.

TOP: Dave Whiting and a basket full of pigs at Waiau. This 224lb Boar was bathing in a sheep trough and outwore his welcome.
BOTTOM: John Whiting with me at Culverden.

CHOOSE YOUR COMPANIONS CAREFULLY

TOP: Brothers John and Dave Whiting. First class hunters. RIGHT: A nice silver grey boar with good tusks. BOTTOM: Dave Whiting with another basket full of pigs.

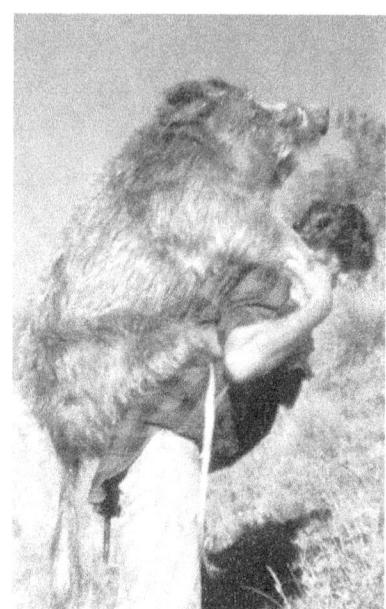

TOP: More good boars.
BOTTOM LEFT: Good hunting country. RIGHT: John Whiting at Culverden.

TOP: Dave Whiting, Robert Mason and me at Culverden.
BOTTOM: John Whiting and me carrying a pig in tandem (not quite steep enough).

CHAPTER 5

Woodchester

ABOUT FIFTY YEARS AGO JACK Barker, Dan Robin and myself decided one Christmas that as the weather was settled, we would walk out to the back boundary of a farm property in North Canterbury, camp there for the night, and get a really early start, to walk further than we ever had before. The animals there would never have been disturbed, and we knew because of the terrain we wouldn't be carrying anything out. So the mission was really just to search and destroy because the farmer hated pigs – all pigs – after being hospitalised by a large boar his sheep dogs had bailed in the manuka below him. He had dismounted his horse and had gone into the scrub where it had attacked and badly injured him. But it wasn't all bad, because while in hospital he met his future wife who was a nursing sister.

Anyway, we got a good head start by sleeping out on the fern for the first night. Dan had a new .222 rifle, which he wanted to try out, so when he sighted three deer he tried his gun out successfully, and killed all three of them. We then scrambled down into a large deep valley with very steep sides. The further down we went the more pigs we came across, until in the creek amongst the fuchsias it sounded like a stockyard with the crashing and thundering of hooves on the creek bed. When the dogs got a pig, at first the other pigs not realising the danger would only run about a hundred metres before they stopped, and started rooting around again.

Looking back up the hill the pigs we had disturbed were going in all different directions like Hornby trains across the face of the hill, some running from right to left, and others left to right, a dozen or more pigs at a time. The dogs had a ball going from pig to pig. It was a massacre. We exhausted ourselves, and later in the day when we were trying to get out of the valley, we came across more pigs every time we sat down. On one stop we nearly sat on top of a pig nest, which was occupied. Pigs chew tussocks and grass, and turn it into straw to make a large bed, and then burrow underneath to keep warm and protect their young. As we reached the top of the main ridge which would take us home, the dogs ran into still more pigs, which promptly took off down the other side with the dogs in pursuit. It was getting late, so we called them off and continued on our way. I don't think any of the pigs were shot, just the deer, but our total for the day was twenty-seven pigs and three deer. You would understand why from then on the area was referred to by us hunters as "Death Valley"!

A year or so later a couple of the locals hunted the area and used packhorses to bring the animals out to the game-packers, so they would have done quite nicely money-wise.

The manager of this farm we hunted was talking to Dan in the local pub one evening and confessed that he had never been that far back on the property, so wouldn't have known what it was like out there. On another trip close to this area I was with a friend, John Roberts to whom I had sold a pup from my old bulldog, Jean, while I had kept two for myself. I had an XR 500 Honda motorcycle, which I rode out to the highest point. As we arrived we saw fresh rooting, so we decided to walk down through the thick matagouri, keeping about fifty metres apart. We had only just started out downhill, when the dogs were on to a good boar right between us. What a sight, a good boar in full flight downhill, with three twelve-months old pups and their mother after him. They could have been forgiven if they had had lost him on such a steep face, but no such worries. Jean hit the boar in the rear and he made a fatal mistake by spinning around as the pups grabbed and held him, so I quickly stuck him.

Luckily we had the bike, so tying the boar's back legs to the left-side foot pegs and draping his carcass over the seat, I started an exciting all downhill journey trying to stop myself being pushed up on to the petrol tank. Despite some hairy moments I arrived safely back at the farm with the pig while John walked back. I was so happy with my pups. They are a great cross those bulldog, bull terrier and greyhound mixtures.

A tip for hunters carrying a big pig in steep country: The steeper the better, no good if too flat. If the only way out is straight up, and you have someone with you; to gain height, get the pig on your shoulders with the back legs hanging down. Get uphill of your mate, and have him put his head between the back legs of the pig and hold on to your belt. It is like being in 4WD and is a lot easier, because you are sharing the weight of the pig. This is an ideal position for a short nuggetty person if he is at the back.

One cold dismal winter's day with the ground covered in snow, Dan and I decided we would not let the weather put us off, so with our dogs Hutch, Saki, Dinda and Scamp in tow and dressed in our thickest and heaviest woollen clothing we set off and headed for the hills. We both wore old World War II army coats, which were common in those days and very popular with motor cyclists. Dan carried his .303 while I elected to look after the dogs as usual.

Heading up a valley, we were having a discussion about which way to go. The ground across the creek from us was covered in low fern, just the same as it was on our side, but rose more steeply. Dan was saying we should cross over, but I was arguing against this saying, "The higher we go the deeper the snow, and surely the pigs would not be up there." While we were talking the dogs had crossed over and headed off uphill.

A short time later they were chasing a pig of about sixty pounds, which they soon caught and held, but because the hill was so steep

they kept sliding downhill closer and closer to the creek, which the lot of them then tumbled into! I got down there and found them all swimming around in a four-foot deep pool at the bottom of a little waterfall. I didn't want to get any wetter than I had to, so decided to lean over and get a grip of the pig's back leg and drag it up and out. Unfortunately the tree root I had a firm grip on was not strong enough to support our combined weights. It came away in my hand, and I did a perfect swallow dive and ended up being totally submerged for a moment before regaining my feet to stand in waist deep water with snow all around. The cold took my breath away.

I killed and gutted the pig where it was, but had to call for assistance from Dan to get out of the pool. The pig and the dogs had to be passed up one at a time. Before Dan came down, I had heard one rifle shot so assumed that he had killed another pig, so asked him what he had shot at. His reply was not what I had expected, He said "I was walking through the fern when I heard one of the dogs come up behind me, so I gave a whistle, then a second one, turned around, and there was a bloody great boar behind me." I said "Did you get it?" He said, "I got such a fright when it rushed past, I fired my rifle in the air."

By this time I had the pig up the hill where I had started, I was soaked to the skin, and my old army coat weighed a ton. I dared not take it off, as the water inside was still a lot warmer than the air on the outside. The journey back to the car was quick, and some warm dry clothes made me feel like a new person.

176lb Boar the day I went out on the bike with John Roberts.

Woodchester: Sam Saunders with a gnat load of pig.

ON MENDIP

On another day Dan, Alan and I were heading out to the back of Woodchester with our dogs on a good clear morning when we heard dogs barking over the boundary fence, on Mendip Hills, and guessed they were out pig hunting. The dogs barked for several minutes without any shots being fired, then it would go quiet for a while till eventually the barking would resume in a different place, only to die out again.

This continued off and on for half an hour or more without any shots being fired, until I realised I hadn't seen my finder, Nero, for a while. I guessed that Nero would have gone to the barking because it was loud and clear, so I decided to head over there to reclaim him.

Of course my half-bulldog Sooty came with me, and as we headed across a ferny face the barking started up again below us in heavy manuka, down in a creek. Sooty was with me up till this point, but I let him go and a pig began to squeal, followed by a rifle shot, then a yelp from a dog. I first thought that these people had hit Sooty to get him off the pig. When I got down into the creek I found three men with a black pig, and several sheep dogs, but I did not see Sooty nor Nero.

Dan, who had followed me over and was in the fern high above us, said he could hear the exchange and the air was blue with expletives when I was told to go, and telling me that if my dogs were any good they would find me.

What really got me upset was when I left I went uphill to where there was another man with a packhorse and I found Sooty attached to a manuka bush by two dog-collars. By this time I was really angry. The guy with the horse was apologetic, and swore he had nothing to do with it, the others stayed down in the creek while I gave them an earful and told them what I thought of them. As I released my dog, my other dog Nero reappeared. I suspect the old finder was too cunning to be caught by a stranger. Within a minute of heading out, my two dogs had a large sow within a hundred and fifty yards of the horse on the same face, an easy one for the other hunters, but after what they had done, I was not feeling very charitable so quickly killed it, didn't bother gutting it, just got the dogs off it and headed back into Woodchester. If they had had half a brain between them they could have had all the pigs they wanted by being civil and honest with me. Nero and Sooty between them would have got them all the pigs they could carry. Instead they chose the other path and got caught out. Up until Sooty had arrived they hadn't acquired one pig.

I had noticed Sooty's nose had a bump on it half way up the snout, and assumed that he had been struck to get him off the pig. Later that day the dogs got on to a good grey boar around one hundred and seventy pounds. When I approached from below, Sooty had a good grip on an ear. I had only just grabbed a leg, when he let it go, which was completely out of character for him. I realized then that something was wrong. When I got back to Christchurch I took him straight to my vet who found Sooty was very lucky to be alive, he had been shot through the nose and had lost all of his top front teeth between the fangs. How he wasn't killed was a miracle, and I was lucky I had taken him to the vet, as there was a grass seed in the hole. Why anyone would want to shoot a hundred pound sow with a dog holding it, I will never know. Obviously they didn't identify the target, or were scared of pigs, or a bit of both.

Woodchester pigs.

TOP LEFT: Father and son, Warwick and Glen Broadhurst. RIGHT: Daniel at Woodchester. BOTTOM LEFT: Me at Woodchester. RIGHT: Neil Stiff and John Tilly.

TOP LEFT: John Roberts with the 176lb boar we brought out on the bike.
RIGHT: John Tilly at Woodchester. BOTTOM: Another haul of Woodchester pork.

CHAPTER 6

Accidents and Mishaps

IN THE EARLY 60s I had a part-time job at Whiting and Waltho's, a Christchurch motorcycle dealership. We were agents for Matchless Vincent James Puch and NSU. I had loved bikes since an early age and when the shop became Honda agents it put me in contact with farmers looking at buying the new farm bike range.

One such contact was J. Douglas-Clifford of Motonau in whom I was immediately interested in, as my cousin, an agricultural contractor in that area had been seeing pigs from his dozer while working at his farm. I asked permission to hunt his land. Eventually a day was arranged, so Dan Robin, Sam Saunders, Keith Churcher and myself, along with our dogs Saki, Hutch, Prince and Patch the latter being a bully pointer-cross spayed female I had recently purchased. We headed for the area we were told to hunt. None of us had been there before, and we were surprised to find there were deep canyons and clay cliffs where, once you had got into the creek, it was difficult to get out of. Poor Patch got herself into difficulties by getting on to what looked like a track, but which petered out about twenty feet above the stony creek bed. By the time she realised, she slipped and fell, landing flat on her back on the stones below. I thought she would have been badly injured if not killed, but she picked herself up and continued as if nothing had happened. She was a tough old girl. Plenty of dogs have died in similar circumstances.

All the land round about was covered in mature pine forest, and we decided to get out of the canyons and hunt amongst the trees. About six feet from the top the clay became too steep for the dogs to get up unassisted, so we dragged Hutch up first and pushed him over the rim. A few seconds later there was a big deep bailing bark a few feet from our heads. We looked at one another in disbelief. Couldn't be, surely not, but it was! We had pushed Hutch over the top and into bed with a good-sized Motonau boar that surprisingly hadn't heard us coming. By this time we were feeling very pleased with ourselves, and all that was needed was to take turns with what should be a relatively easy carry back to the car. We hadn't had to chase the pig, as it had never moved from his bed. Hutch had kept his attention until given the command to hold him while he was dispatched.

The carry-out should have taken no more than twenty to thirty minutes, but after an hour we were still in the trees. Suddenly Dan said, "We are going around in circles!" "Nah, don't believe that," said I. "Well, what's that then?" he asked, pointing at the ground, and there lying in a neat pile was the pig guts we had left an hour before. To say we were surprised would be putting it mildly. How one of us at least hadn't picked up on it sooner I'll never know, but we learnt from that. It is not uncommon to go around in circles in forests where no landmarks are visible. Humans are known to have a tendency to walk in circles when lost especially when conditions are cloudy or they are in a forest. Luckily we didn't make the same mistake twice. The pig was one hundred and sixty-six pounds gutted.

On another occasion, while hunting on my own at Oxford one

morning, the mist was low and the undergrowth was covered in drops of moisture so it wasn't long before I was soaked from the knees down and the dogs started to look more like drowned rats. We climbed up through the lower paddocks, and then through the native bush, until eventually we gained the ridge, which was parallel with the main road where we were amongst the clouds. The breeze was behind us coming up the hill so I decided to walk along the tops for a while. The bush was quite open, and the ground beneath, undulating. Every now and again there would be a short break in the clouds and a brief glimpse of blue sky, so I decided to climb a tree to try and see where I was as I had been walking for quite a while without coming across anything interesting. As I climbed higher, sure enough there came a break in the clouds just long enough to see a clearing a few hundred metres ahead. I knew that all I had to do to get back to the car was to drop down to my left, because the road was on my left – so I thought.

I decided to walk as far as the clearing, so set off once again with renewed vigour while the dogs skirted around looking for fresh scent. After about half an hour I still hadn't arrived at the clearing I had seen, and realised something was wrong. So once again I found a tree to climb and waited for another break in the clouds. When the break finally came I was quite shocked, as everywhere I looked there was nothing to be seen but thick bush; every direction you looked, unending bush. If I had gone downhill to my left, thinking I was returning to the car I would have been in trouble. I did the only thing I could do. I very cautiously retraced my footsteps back the way I came, being very careful not to go astray. Thinking about it later I think that although my journey felt and appeared to be fairly straight, it obviously was not, and I had actually travelled on the ridge in a horseshoe shape, thus taking me away from the car and the road if I had been unlucky enough to try going out that way (to my left).

At eleven p.m. one evening while lying in bed listening to the late news on the radio I learned that a group of young people had gone for a walk up the Waterfall Track, and one of them had failed to return to their car. I was due to go hunting in the same area next morning, and was very familiar with the terrain, so thinking we could be useful I rang Dan to see if he would come with me, but he wasn't interested, so I drove up alone.

Arriving at the car park area at about twelve thirty a.m. I found a police car and a policeman and the lost girl's father inside. We had a chat. I wanted to have a look on the far side of the hill. I could envisage what had happened and knew from experience how easy it was to become disoriented. I had brought along a couple of torches and a flask of tea. There was not a breath of wind. So it was an ideal night to find a lost person. I spoke briefly to the couple in the police car, told them I was prepared to go up the hill and said I reckoned I had a good chance of a successful outcome. It was then we all went to Judson's farmhouse where a command centre had been established. After a bit of mucking around they decided they didn't want me to go up there because I might disturb any scent, and they were concerned about what I might find. I was fairly sure that I knew what had happened and the girl would be ok. They were getting ready for a full-scale search the next morning.

Not looking for her that night, as it turned out, was a mistake. This was a dead calm night without a breath of wind. Sound would travel. There was a better chance of finding her than not. When hunting, the noises generated on the plains below can be clearly heard if there is no wind when climbing the hill. Roosters crowing, tractors working, and unseen animal noises a long way off are clearly heard, but you couldn't hear your dogs fifty yards away on the same hill if there was a curve in the terrain. Knowing all this, and in perfect conditions, I was a little disappointed to be sent home again.

Next day I kept listening for any news on how the search was

PORKERS

TOP: Marlborough Sounds. BOTTOM: Maurie Smith.

Sam and me with a 166 lbs Motonau Boar we carried in a circle for an hour.

progressing. By about four p.m. I phoned the central police station to ask if the girl had been found, and was told she hadn't. I told the woman on the other end of the phone where I thought she would be and as it turned out I was correct, She had turned around a couple of times and chose the wrong way down, taking herself into real tiger country. I was told later that she was found by a person driving on the Lees Valley Road. She was sitting on a rock in the middle of the Ashley River. All's well that ends well.

Don't ever be embarrassed to use maps and compasses, or nowadays GPS – some day you could need them.

ENDEAVOUR INLET

Maurie Smith, a very good pig-hunting mate of mine, worked for the New Zealand Police and he was strongly built, easy to get along with, and made to be a packhorse, never shirking if there was a load to be carried.

I was fortunate enough to have been given the opportunity to use another friend's bach at Endeavour Inlet in the Marlborough Sounds, so Maurie and I decided that as he had a boat to get us out there, and I had the dogs and a place to stay, we would do a three day trip to the Inlet. Endeavour Inlet is a beautiful place with baches scattered throughout the bush-clad hills with a good walking track below the baches but above the beach which leads to Furneaux Lodge, where many a good night has been spent by the locals amidst the outstanding scenery.

Everything seemed handily placed, a ten minute walk to the pub, and even fresh pig-sign not hard to find. Anyway, I am getting a bit ahead of myself. To tow Maurie's boat we really should have had a large car or a 4WD, but I had a 1973 Datsun 180 B, and being a Datsun fan, had no doubt that towing a weight far in excess of the weight of the car and contents would be a breeze. Maurie was not so sure, and a bit dubious. His seventeen foot six inch glass-over-ply cabin cruiser was loaded to capacity and filled with our food and beer, dog food, and seventy litres of outboard fuel, and all the other things you think you might need but seldom do, plus four dogs in a cage.

We arrived at Picton without any problems, launched the boat, and made our way to the inlet without getting lost. After settling in and a quick coffee, it was on with the boots and away hunting. We climbed the hill behind the bach, and made our way along the ridge until we were directly above the lodge. The ground was very open under the large native trees, and visibility could have been as much as fifty metres. All of a sudden one of the dogs started to bark, while almost at the same instant, the barking stopped and a pig of about one hundred and twenty pounds flew past me. I would swear that its feet were not touching the ground. It went over the brow of the hill and was gone in an instant. I was stunned, I thought at the time I had never seen a pig move so quickly, and I was very disappointed it had given the dogs the slip. So we adjourned to the bach for the rest of that day.

The next day we decided to try another area across the inlet which was covered in thick fern and seemed to be uninhabited. How wrong can you be? Shortly after landing we were confronted by an irate farmer who asked, "Do you want your dogs shot now, or shall I leave it till later?" He explained that he had had trouble with dogs in the past and had put an ad in the local paper saying any dogs found on his property would be shot. Fair enough, we were in the wrong and apologized for our mistake. So we departed on reasonable terms and headed back the way we had come. Maurie dropped the dogs and me at the foot of a rocky spur at the head of the inlet, and we arranged to meet at the same spot a few hours later. As I climbed up the scrub and manuka hill I found there was a well-worn track and

I hadn't gone far when the dogs started barking ahead of me and to my left, which led to an area the pigs had been living in. (Where the pigs hadn't cleared it, the fern was six feet high.)

About five feet inside the thickest part the dogs by this time had hold of a boar which was dragging them downhill. The boar thrashed his head from side to side, cutting a track for himself with his tusks as I stood, bayonet in hand, waiting at the bottom for his appearance – which was not long in coming, First the tip of his snout, then the rest of his head, with his beady eyes fixed on me. The dogs had been left behind, and the boar and I were face to face and eye to eye.

I had the heel of the bayonet held down at ground level as I tried to get under his neck to deliver a fatal blow, but without success. As I struck, so did he, knocking my wrist to one side. I remember wondering if I had been ripped, but couldn't take my eyes away from his to have a look.

As he emerged from the fern, I shuffled backwards, my feet becoming entangled in the fern roots, and I fell over on to my back. My first thoughts were, "This is how you get hurt, you've gotta get off the track!" I corkscrewed and rolled to one side, allowing the boar to get by. I scrambled to my feet, and by this time the dogs had arrived. About thirty feet downhill they stopped and held the pig while I finished him off. It was then that I noticed blood on the fern that wasn't from the pig, and I was dismayed to discover that Bonnie had been struck in the jugular by a tusk. There was nothing I could do to save her.

Maurie was not due back for another hour or so, and there were no vets for miles anyway. All I could do was comfort her and hold her while she died. All this, for a mangy little one hundred and twenty-five pounder, although a lot of dogs have been killed by pigs of this size. I think the dogs tend to under-estimate the danger when they are used to seeing much larger pigs. I felt very upset about losing a really good

TOP: Waiau: Alan Orchard and me. The day was too hot and this pig was too big to carry out. BOTTOM: But not too big to carry for a trophy snap.

TOP: A deer shot by Daniel at Oxford. BOTTOM: A deer shot at Oxford.

dog, but these are the risks you take when hunting. My only consolation was that Bonnie had loved hunting, and had been out on many exciting sorties with me, and she had had a good life. Any time a dog goes missing for an extended period of time you wonder if you will ever see them again. At least I knew what had happened to Bonnie.

A CLOSE CALL

One day while hunting the hills on the highest point at my Murchison haunt, the dogs were working in some bush below us when there was a bark from their direction. I jumped up and put my feet into gear before my brain, charging off through the scrub with my head down and with my eyes half shut. I didn't want to lose an eye. Too late I realized my mistake when I ran straight off a bluff!

I was in mid-air and thought, "Help, I have done it this time, I am going to break my legs." Luckily I landed on the branch of a tree, which broke my fall as I grabbed it, and sliding down the branches the tree lowered me to within touching distance of the ground. I was safe. This was a lucky escape. I could just as easily have been impaled on an upward pointing branch or, equally fatally, have missed the tree entirely and slammed into the ground.

A similar accident occurred out on the Clarence Reserve when I was standing on a hill, which was covered in burnt manuka. Burnt manuka is very sharp to push your way through. One of my dogs barked down the bottom of the hill, and I took off immediately with my head down and ran straight into a sharp piece of stick cutting open my scalp. Talk about stuck pigs bleeding, I could hardly see for the blood running down my face and into my eyes, but there was no use worrying about it because we were in the area for a few days hunting and couldn't just leave. My wound healed itself ok without any attention, and we carried on hunting.

SCAMP

Every pig hunter at some stage while training his or her dogs has the odd mishap, and Scamp the foxy was a troublemaker from the city. He had been someone's pet, and lived opposite the Islington freezing works in Christchurch where he got himself into trouble for chasing sheep. Not a good start in life for him, but the final straw was when he bit the postman. He was either going to be put down or someone had to give him a home or a hobby, so I took him for a pig dog. I didn't really want to take him at the time because I had Dinda, and he was another little snarly mongrel, so I gave Scamp to my friend Diesel Dan.

Scamp had one of those small dog complexes; little dogs sometimes attack as the best means of defence especially if they have a gang of tough guys behind them – sort of like saying, "Do you want to fight me, brother?" When he saw big animals he wasn't frightened, and he took a lot of disciplining to keep under control, but he soon came right, and turned into a good little hunter and covered a lot of country with that three-legged gait that fox terriers are known for.

Scamp was with us when Diesel Dan, Jack Barker and I came over the hill from Glen Colwyn one day. It was beautiful weather, a clear April day after a frost, and we headed down towards the sea. We walked down a broad valley and noticed a mob of cattle on the far side of the hill to our right. As we looked, a big stag jumped up and ran off uphill through the fern away from them. The side of the valley we were on was fern covered with a little bit of scrub in the gullies, and when we went to come back, we came up the side where we had seen the stag earlier, and where the cattle were. Sometimes pigs hang around near cattle, turning over cowpats and looking for worms.

We had nearly arrived up to where we saw the stag, when Scamp started bailing in some thick fern. It was a cattle beast about fifty metres away in a bit of a gully. I hadn't seen it straight away. I raced up there, but by the time I arrived the cattle beast had a dog on each ear and was facing downhill. I was really worked up by then, roaring at the dogs. I kicked one dog off on the near side and leaned over the neck of the beast, punching the other dog in the nose to

get him off. They all let it go, and I was left with my arm around the neck of the animal which was by then bolting down through the fern into a gully and carrying me into a small glen under some fuchsia trees where the dogs grabbed it once again. By this time I was hysterical and blew my dentures out into the mud! I found myself in front of the cow, which didn't appreciate that I was trying to help, and as I was trying to retrieve my teeth from out of the dirt and debris, every time I put my head down the cow charged at me. I tried to grab it around the head again, and each time I did, it butted me and shunted me up the hill.

Eventually it managed to make its escape and I kept the dogs back, but they were determined to go after it again, so as soon as I retrieved my teeth and had turned around they had the cattle beast again further up the hill. It was strange, because it was just this one cow that they worried, so I always wondered if the cow associated too closely with the stag and had acquired some of its scent on it. Scamp had been the instigator. He was the one who had set the dogs on to the cow. He and the other dogs were given a good hiding and never looked at any more cattle. At least not that day anyway.

Sometimes when you are on someone's farm the owner will ask you to give a hand, with a little farm work and it is the least you can do when you when you are given free access to the hunting and game, so when my friend Mike asked me to give him a hand to draft some sheep I was only too pleased to help. While standing in the yards I noticed a dirty great ram standing close by in the pen where I stood operating the gates. After about half an hour Mike thoughtfully turned around to me and said, "I'm surprised he hasn't gone for you yet!" I hadn't given the ram a second thought and had completely ignored it. It was then that Mike told me it had been in a small paddock in town, which the local schoolchildren used to cut through for a short-cut until the ram started flattening them, and he had expected it to try it with me and seemed to be very disappointed. I guess that was also one of my lucky days.

DOMETT DAZE

During my travels I have come across many hard case characters but none so unpredictable as one particular guy. It was a beautiful clear summer morning when suddenly the old V8 started to wander all over the road. I knew immediately it was a puncture so I stopped. Unfortunately, a few days before, I had lost the wheel brace on the cemetery bend just north of Cheviot. We had tied the boot down and put a sack in it to stop it from shutting completely in order to get air in for the dogs that travelled in the boot. We heard the wheel brace hit the tar seal, then skid across the surface of the road and into the long grass at the roadside. Despite spending ten minutes searching we never found it, so had no way to remove the wheel.

Being only about half a mile south of the Domett store, I volunteered to go to try and borrow some tools. As I approached the store, I noticed a black German shepherd-cross on a long running wire. The dog barked and growled a bit, so I just told it to shut up, gave it a pat and continued to the back door. The time was about six a.m. with the sun well up as I knocked on the back door. A very angry looking man eventually opened it, and he proceeded to give a tirade of abuse. "You bloody mongrels, waking me up. I have only just got to bed at two o'clock, and I don't need to be woken up at this hour." I was taken aback. When he learned I was only there to borrow some tools, he exploded again. "I am not in the business of lending tools, and anyway nobody ever bothers to return them!"

After a tirade lasting about five minutes, I was resigned to failure in my quest for help, and was about to take my departure when he did a complete about turn and decided to be helpful after all. He fetched his tools, and said, "Oh, would you like some fruit, here, I have bananas and apples, whatever you like, and while you are here you had better take a spare tube in case you get another puncture."

I duly returned to the car, changed the wheel, and returned the tools. The shop owner could not have been friendlier. He told me that if I ever needed anything after hours to just call in and he would serve us. "Don't be afraid to call in any time," he said, "no problem, anytime!"

So it was a few months later during the winter we were heading home to Christchurch from Kaikoura and were a bit low on fuel. We were nearing Dommet, where the store owner lived, so I told Dan, "This guy is a friend of mine, he has a petrol pump, let's fill the car up here." It was about nine p.m. and dark, and although the lights were off in the shop I could see them still burning in the living quarters. As we pulled up the lights suddenly went off. As I approached the dog on the running wire, it stopped barking and lay with its head on its outstretched front paws with its tail wagging, and I bent down to give it a pat. It suddenly snarled, and leapt up, hitting me in the chest and knocking me out of its reach, and then proceeded to do a good imitation of a guard dog. He was all teeth, and resembled a crocodile. I recoiled and was most annoyed, considering for a moment setting my dogs on to it to teach it a lesson, but thought better of it. We could have started a war.

I heard later that the storeowner had had problems with break-ins. He was reputed to have sneaked around to the front of his shop one night, shotgun in hand, to find a person on their knees at the front door trying to pick the lock. After a warning that he was about to get both barrels if he could still see him by the time he counted five. It was said that the would-be thief disappeared rapidly.

I never did make contact with the storeowner again, but often wondered how he was and if things had worked out well for him in the end, and if he kept taking his pills!

DOVE HUTT

A friend, Chris Coy, had arranged a weekend away with a trip to the Dove Hut on a north Canterbury farm. For the previous few days the weather had been terrible, strong freezing cold southerlies with snow in the foothills. The only two things we had going for us were that the forecast was for showers clearing the following day, and as we had to walk over a range of hills to get there we had the cold winds at our backs. There wasn't much point in starting early, so we didn't get mov-

ACCIDENTS AND MISHAPS

Daniel and his children.

TOP: Pig hunters Daniel Robin, Sam Saunders and unknown, with Mickey Foster in a crouching position. BOTTOM: Deer head found at bottom of a virtually inaccessible waterfall at Waiau.

ACCIDENTS AND MISHAPS

TOP: Maurie Smith, Alan Orchard and me.
BOTTOM: Mt Palm: Robert Mason, Dave Whiting and unknown with dogs Percival and Ricky.

ing till mid-morning. Our dogs were Ricky, the staghound springer spaniel-cross, and Tim, out of the bulldog, Jean, and littermate, Bee, also fathered by Rick. From the pound I had taken a likely looking black and tan Doberman-cross bull terrier. We crested the first range of hills without incident and the dogs got a fifty-pound pig halfway down the other side, but we didn't see any other game that day.

With several inches of snow on the ground we were looking forward to the warmth and comfort of the hut, and with darkness fast approaching and visibility of about fifty metres, we arrived. We were dismayed to find that all that remained was a charred mess of corrugated iron and burned timber sitting on a concrete floor where the hut had once stood. We quickly formed the sheets of iron into a teepee shape after scraping the snow off the ground first, and then gathered some manuka to light a fire in the middle. Our sleeping bags were quite damp but being of good quality and feather-filled, surrounded by our dogs, we still had a reasonable sleep in our makeshift shelter without which we could not have survived as we could not have slept in the open.

Thankfully next morning dawned bright and clear. For once the forecast had been right so after a hearty breakfast and a cuppa or two we gathered our gear and dogs and headed up a likely looking hill. Just before the top, we came across some fresh rooting which had been done that night and the dogs disappeared over the ridge into a thick matagouri face. The new dog let out a yelp and came back to me at the same time as the others started to bail so I guess he was a bit confused about what steps he should take when he met the boar, so decided to retreat. He didn't do anything wrong, he just needed time and work.

A short while later I had shot and gutted a decent boar, when I heard the sound of a helicopter just below the ridge over which we had come. Peeping over the ridge I found I was almost at eye-level with the pilot who had been having a close look at the fresh sign. It was Bill Atkinson from Woodbank Station with his mate Bill Hales and, as he set one skid down on the ridge, he yelled out, "Where's your truck? We will take it out for you."

His kind offer was gratefully accepted and after slinging the pig beneath the chopper we watched, whooping and hollering as it disappeared into the distance, leaving a trail of blood as it left. We were ecstatic. It couldn't have worked out better. We were miles from our car, and at around one hundred and eighty-pound, it would most likely have been beyond our capabilities to carry it that distance and to scale the hills that needed to be traversed.

We found out later the hut had been burned down because a couple of young hunters failed to extinguish their fire properly before leaving the camp. On a sad note, both Bills were pilots and were eventually killed in separate chopper accidents. I believe at least one hit wires across a river.

I gave the Doberman bull terrier cross to a young guy who worked on the farm. The dog was not chained up and allowed to run loose at night so the inevitable happened, and while at large it killed a sheep and was not given a second chance. The boss insisted it was shot. It was still not the dog's fault. It needed training. We got back to our car without having to lose any unnecessary sweat, went down to where the pig lay, threw him on to the trailer, then we were off to the game buyers. Easy money for a change.

CHAPTER 7

Lessons Learned

EARLY ONE FINE AND FROSTY winter's morning Alan Orchard, Dan Robin and I arrived at Tony's farm at Waiau after a two-hour drive from Christchurch. We left Alan's Mercedes, heading for one of our favourite places. The ground and matagouri bushes were still frozen stiff as the three of us strode purposefully up a hill. The freezing cold air invigorated our lungs.

At the time I was sporting a brand-new Green River skinning-knife complete with leather pouch, so chose to leave my bayonet at home. However, a skinning knife with its broad curved blade is made for a specific purpose and definitely not meant for pig sticking.

We hadn't gone more than a kilometre when the dogs grabbed a sixty-pound sow down in a small gully, so I went down to stick it thinking 'this is a good start to the day'. Why I tried to stick the pig with my left hand I will never know. I am right-handed, but I did. My hands were frozen and damp as I took a stab at the pig's heart area and promptly struck a rib causing my had to slip up the handle of the knife slightly, so getting another good firm grip I let rip with a good powerful blow, only to find I had struck a rib for the second time, only this time my fingers slid up the blade cutting three of them to the bone.

I cursed loudly, killing the pig, and after a quick discussion with my mates I decided I would continue; after all we had hardly started. If I could inflict it surely I could stand a little bit of pain. As I climbed the hill my heart rate increased and so did the throbbing pain in my fingertips, and by the time I reached the ridge I had made up my mind to seek medical attention and get some stitches.

There was now a problem: the boys wanted me to drive myself out to Cheviot but the farm had several gates which had to be opened and closed by hand meaning you first had to stop, get out of the car, open the gate, find a stick or other object to hold it open, drive through, stop, get out and make sure each of the gates shut properly and drive on to the next of about eight or more gates. The last thing I wanted to do was to damage Alan's Mercedes with a gate shutting while halfway through. Then after visiting the doctor the process would have to be repeated as I returned to the farm for my friends. Anyway Alan took pity and relented, taking me to an after-hours stitcher-upperer in Cheviot – might even have been the vet for all I cared.

I watched as the doctor took a large needle from his collection, threaded it with cat-gut and asked if I wanted a painless injection, saying it was just another prick, so being a big brave pig-hunter I declined. But my eyes stuck out a bit when he started about half an inch back gave a powerful thrust and the needle came right out through the end of the first finger then tied it in a knot.

"Thank God there are only two more to come." I thought. The wounds healed quickly and cleanly but I never regained the full feeling in those fingers and I never used a skinning knife to stick a pig again.

SPOOKED

I quite often hunted alone, with just the dogs and me, and must admit I did enjoy the company of the dogs and peace of the bush and countryside. One evening, while staying at the hut at Murchison, I decided to get an extra early start the next day. I would arrive at daybreak five kilometres away at an open fern-covered valley where the hunting was good. I woke up at four thirty a.m. and it was pitch black. My two dogs, Ricky the liver and white spaniel staghound-cross, and Spook, a black bulldog-cross, were keen to get going. I had forgotten to bring a torch, and the track though the bush was wet and boggy with all sorts of hidden obstacles. As I started off I had to regularly call the dogs in, as they wanted to hunt.

It was not long before they got on to a scent and shot off to the left of me into the bush and up the hill followed by a burst of barking, then a period of heavy breathing signifying they had grabbed a boar. The first thing I did was run face-first into a tree while I fumbled my way through the undergrowth. Before I was halfway to the battle the pig broke. About this time I came across a large fallen tree, which spanned a small gully, so decided to walk across it to the ridge opposite me. As I arrived on the other side I stopped and listened. It was quiet for a minute, and then I heard one of my dogs coming down from above me. As he stood six feet in front of me, in the middle of the track puffing like a steam train, I said to him, "Where did the pig go, Spook?" While I was having this conversation with him, suddenly there was a snort and a crash as this black object hurtled past me and crashed its way down the hill through the debris and fallen branches.

I had been talking to the boar. After that I was careful to keep the dogs at heel until I reached my intended destination. There I got a good eating-sized sow and returned to the hut for a feed and a rest, quite satisfied.

If you ever asked Tony Gardiner from Woodchester Farm if he knew where any pigs were he would give you his stock standard answer, "Pigs are where you find them."

It was good experience finding out for one's self by doing the hard yards and covering the country. You soon learn that if you get a big boar in a dense patch of scrub the chances are he would be replaced within a week or two by another big boar, and this was the case with an area at the end of Gardiner's Flat paddocks.

Many years ago the manuka on a terrace above the river had been cut, and left where it lay until eventually the regrowth combined with the fallen mat to become almost impenetrable; a haven for boars. But one day while skirting this area, which covers about one hectare, Dinda was hunting just ahead of me when suddenly he started to bark at a clump of lawyer which was within a few feet of the thick cover.

Before Hutch and Saki could get there the boar made a break for it, straight into the manuka and gone, with the dogs in hot pursuit. I struggled to follow them, sometimes walking on top of the matted vegetation, sometimes slipping off, and sometimes finding myself straddling sticks while waist deep, and struggling to drag myself up again. By this time things had gone pretty quiet so I decided to get down inside the matted vegetation and make use of the pig tunnels. As I slid feet first down a slight incline I suddenly realized that I wasn't alone! Where I could see a bit of daylight before, it had gone black, and an animal raced up the tunnel towards me.

My heart skipped a couple of beats and a large black possum ran up the length of my body and over my face and head. Eventually the

tunnel took me to the edge of a clay cliff, which had a well-worn track zig-zagging its way to the river below. I listened, and I could hear the dogs doing battle with the pig half way up a bush gully directly opposite. So quickly running down, and then up into the bush I soon had another nice boar around one hundred and sixty pounds.

I was sitting at home early one warm Sunday afternoon when the phone rang. It was Mervin, a keen young guy I had met who owned a young half bulldog-cross he was training and he wanted me to go hunting with him up at Oxford, about an hour's drive from home. I wasn't that keen as it was a bit late in the day for my liking. I like to get there before daybreak. I tried my best to talk him out of it but he was persistent and in the end I gave in, so went and gathered our dogs Hutch, Saki, Roy and Tipper. I think Mervin's dog was called Max.

We arrived at the hunting place around three p.m. released the dogs, and headed up into the gorse, which turned to native bush higher up the hill. There were numerous ruts and gullies along the face, running parallel with the road. The pigs here are tough and hard to catch. After an unsuccessful couple of hours we finally arrived at the highest ridge just as the dogs took off after a mob of deer over the far side which is bush as far as the eye can see. That might have been ok except that at the same time the wind changed to south-west and heavy rain started to fall along with strong winds and we had no choice but to head back down to the shelter of the car. We found a bit of shelter behind some mature macrocarpa trees and got a fire going, huddling around the fire to keep warm while waiting for the dogs who were all still missing. Mervin was adamant he wasn't going anywhere until his dog Max returned. I think the first dog to turn up was Roy, followed by Hutch, then around ten thirty p.m. Max arrived back. Once he had his dog, Mervin wanted to go home. He lost interest in anything else, so at eleven p.m. after notifying the farmer of the two lost dogs we departed for home leaving some clothing behind for the dogs. (If you leave some clothing with your smell on them the dogs will normally stay there until you return.)

I received a phone call two days later. One was back. The last dog was picked up on the fourth day. That was Saki – he came walking across the paddocks where the farmer was working. When I picked him up he was none the worse for his adventures and was very pleased to see me. I don't think I ever went out with Mervin again after that. It was unfortunate we had gone together in his vehicle or I might have waited longer. Always be prepared for the unexpected.

Check weather forecasts and carry a light nylon wind-proof parka tucked in your belt; they weigh nothing and could be a lifesaver. They will turn a good shower when new and help keep your woolen garments dry and best of all – they are windproof!

Tip
In steep rugged country keep out of creeks unless you know where you're going; follow well-used stock and game tracks where possible.

KAIPAPA

A mutual friend of Dan's and mine had a holiday home in the Queen Charlotte Sounds, so when the opportunity arose for a weekend up there, we weren't going to refuse. The weather was cold, with showers and sleet forecast, but nothing was going to deter two keen young hunters with new country to explore. We were running late on the day we arrived and we knew that we had limited daylight because it was winter. Murray, the owner of the property, wasn't interested in hunting, so was staying behind to keep warm.

Dan and I climbed up behind the house until we arrived at the ridge, and then continued to follow it up until we were looking down into what appeared to be a good open ferny face with a likelihood of pigs. Halfway down we caught a little pig, and decided to go on down to the beach we could see in the distance, to walk on back to base. However the beach became less of a good idea the closer we got. The hill dropped off steeply. So steeply in fact that I slipped and fell forward in a freak accident, when a manuka stake passed between my knife-belt and body, leaving me hanging upside down, unable to get free as the belt was an army-world war two web belt which needed the pressure released to undo the buckle.

After a struggle, and some help from Dan, I managed to get free of the manuka stake, but I was glad I wasn't on my own as it could have been a different ending for me, especially if I had lost my knife. When we arrived at the beach, we realized our mistake. The beach was tiny and only led to bluffs, and the terrain changed from fern to heavy mature bush above us.

By this time it was dark, with shower clouds scudding across the sky, and freezing cold, so I suggested to Dan we might have to spend the night out on the hill, but his illogical reply was that he wasn't going to do that because he was scared he would wake up and find himself dead. So Dan wouldn't accept that suggestion at all.

Now, Dan can't swim, and as we made our way around the foot of the bluffs, he panicked. His voice came out of the darkness, "Help, I'm slipping. I'm going in," (to the sea). Thinking I might have to jump in after and rescue him, I was surprised when he landed on a flat rock just under the surface of the water, which was only six inches deep. By this time the dogs were having difficulty following us as we climbed up and over some parts using the scrub and bush as handholds. Prince, the black Labrador, stopped in front of Dan, who accidently gave him a nudge, and pushed him over an unseen drop, poor dog. However Prince survived the ordeal and picked himself up and was soon back with us.

Eventually we got to a point where we could see the lights of the house across the bay, and when we saw the door open and Murray appear on the decking outside, we yelled our loudest. "Come and get us!"

"Get stuffed," was the reply, and he went back inside and shut the door!

We struggled on, and arrived back at the house about ten p.m. minus a few of the dogs, but we went looking for them the next morning as soon as it turned daylight, and boy! were they pleased to see us.

We learnt a lesson that day. We should have retraced our steps up the ferny face to the ridge, and back to the house, but at the time we thought we were doing the right thing. Another lesson we learnt early was not to try coming down creeks in rugged country unless you know it can be done. Invariably you will find waterfalls, and Murphy's Law dictates that the further you go, the bigger and harder to negotiate they can become, and you could end up having to retrace your steps. If you have already carried or assisted your dogs down, you could be in trouble, because the walls can be sheer and moss-covered. Best keep out. Animals aren't stupid, so look for and use game trails where possible.

It takes time to build your fitness for pig hunting. A workmate once asked me if I would take him out hunting. Without giving it much thought, I said to him "I'd better find you somewhere easy to go, because you won't be fit for the hills." His quick reaction was to state that he would go anywhere I went and keep up the pace no trouble., after all he was only 23, several years younger than myself, and a keen jogger, boxer and went to the gym regularly.

We arrived nice and early at Jollybrook, crossed the swing bridge and headed across the flats towards the hills. Jim had brought a friend with him and together they set off at a furious pace, across the matagouri flats towards the hills where there was a steep climb.

I yelled out for them to slow down telling them, "You won't keep up that pace all day." But they scoffed, and reckoned they could, but I had chosen the steepest hill to climb, and before too long they were both feeling exhausted. The sun came up, it got hot, and within two hours the two friends didn't want to go any further. Jim discovered that day he was not as fit as he had thought. He never did say if he enjoyed the day, but never asked to go with me again. It is evident that there are definitely varying degrees of fitness, and our bodies become accustomed to the types of exercise we are doing. I was sure I wouldn't have been any good at football or boxing , but keen pig hunters obviously in time gain their fitness for the hills. I personally reached the stage where it was such an obsession, if I didn't go out and do at least one hard run, I never felt satisfied..

CHAPTER 8

Island Hills

ON ONE OF OUR EARLIER trips into the valley camp, long before we had the Gnat, Arthur Shand – who owned Island Hills station in North Canterbury – kindly lent Dan, Alan, Joe, (a Dutch friend of ours) and me his trusty half-draft packhorse named Steel. At that stage I don't think any of us had had any experience with horses. My own total experience was the rides around a paddock I had when I was ten years old and when the fourteen-year old owner was kindly disposed towards me and let me have a go. I loved that little bay pony. It was then that I decided that my only hope for a pony of my own was to pray for one, so every night before going to sleep, I prayed for a horse, pony, a Clydesdale – anything would do! And it worked, even if it did take thirty years.

Eventually my prayers were answered when, at age forty, a work colleague named Mickey bought a young un-raced standardbred for his daughter as a hack, but then told me she had lost interest in it and asked if I would like it and gave him to me. The horse which had been named "Little Bull" had grown larger than expected, and was too big for his daughter to ride. He had been kept at Mickey's brother's place twenty miles out in the country, and for a young girl without transport it was difficult for her to get there anyway.

I found a paddock next to my friend Joe Crawford's place in Bassett Street, and I thought I would go out and ride the horse home following the Waimakariri River. Arranging somewhere to keep the horse had been easy enough and when I went out to West Melton to see the horse I found he was sixteen point two hands, dark bay, and needed veterinary treatment. He had injured his back leg, entangling it in barbed wire, and it had become infected. So it was a horse-float job. I arranged for a horse float and went out to pick him up, his leg soon healed and in the meantime I bought a saddle and bridle. I should have realized that horses are just like big dogs with all the same characteristics. They can be naughty, affectionate or downright dangerous if you don't know what you are doing. I had not ridden a horse since riding a friend's pony when I was about ten, and here I was at forty with the first horse I had ever owned. So let the games begin!

Eagerly I anticipated great times riding my new horse, but it didn't turn out as easy as I had hoped for. He seemed to know I was novice, and refused to cooperate. He repeatedly dawdled going away from his paddock, always wanting to turn back, and if he got his way he would race home at twice the speed he was doing before! One Saturday I thought I would show the previous owner how clever I was by riding Little Bull out to his home at New Brighton to visit. They didn't know that I had walked halfway there with the horse by leading him, and mounted him just as I approached their house and rode up their drive!

As I left to come home, there was a lot of traffic on the road because it was a Saturday and New Brighton was the only shopping-centre open in the weekends in those days. The horse was very willing to get home, but we had to wait and give way to the traffic at the end of Wainoni Road. Spotting a gap I gave him a nudge to cross the road at the foot of the bridge, and the horse slipped and went down on his knees, picked himself up, and bolted down New Brighton Road towards his paddock, with me leaning back and pulling on the reigns shouting, "Whoa, whoa!" I was afraid he might step into a pot-hole on the grass verge and break a leg. There were people out in the front gardens mowing their lawn standing with their mouths open watching the drama unfold and unable to do anything to help. At last I managed to get him to stop and I jumped straight

off. My knees were knocking a bit by then. I immediately realized I had done the wrong thing, I should have stayed on him, because he would think that he could get me off him every time by bolting.

I acquired a very old book with tips about how to handle horses, and read that when the horse turns to go home and you don't want it to, you let the horse turn, but pull it around till it completes a circle so you are facing the way you originally started from and then try and move forward.

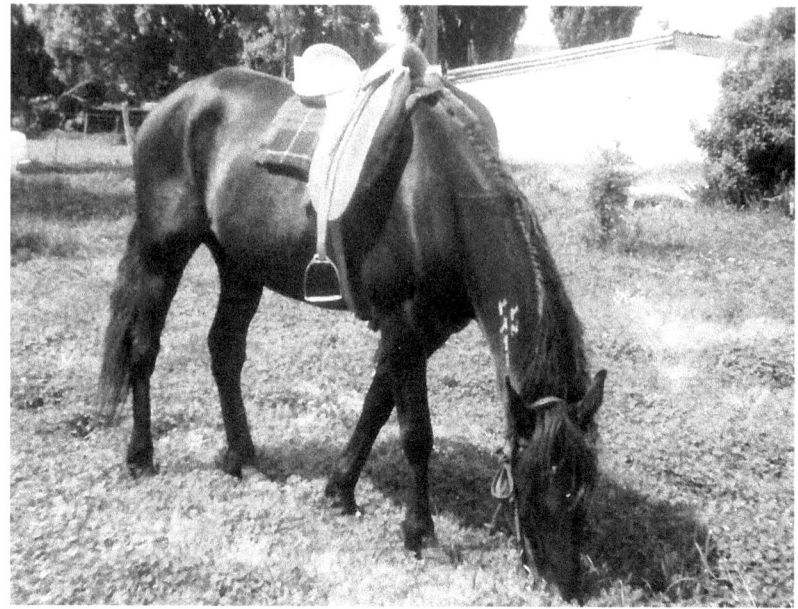

My very special horse, Little Bull.

I always wanted to take Little Bull down to the beach, but he was reluctant to go past Burwood Hospital. One Saturday we had a real argument between us. He had run me close to a barbed wire fence until I took my foot out of the stirrup, then put his head down and galloped flat tack towards home trying to wipe me out under some tree branches that were overhanging the road side. I lay along his side with my arms around his neck like an Indian to avoid the branches. Another bad habit he had was to pig-jump to try and buck me off, but I had a long set of reins and I always carried a stick. When he tried this, I couldn't do anything but lie back in the saddle with the stick flailing in my right arm. This probably encouraged him to buck more, but I only ever came off once and that was on a sawdust track when we were heading for a deep ditch and I bailed out rather than go into a six-foot drain. The cure was simple, but I didn't know it at the time. I wasn't keeping a tight enough rein on him, and that was all it was. He stopped his monkey business when friends pointed this out to me.

We gradually sorted out our differences and thereafter he just improved out of sight and we developed a great understanding, with a mutual respect for one another and became best mates. One time with a couple of friends and their horses we were cantering down Lower Styx Road when I found that I hadn't rechecked my girth strap and the saddle was starting to slip. The others continued on while I stopped, fixed the problem, straightened the saddle blanket, retightened the girth strap and had one foot in the stirrup when we took off flat out again to catch up with the others.

Little Bull turned out to be a great walking horse with a big long stride, he would take the lead and keep going, leaving everyone else in his dust. Other riders would call out, "Hang on, it's not a race," but he was keen and willing. I became really attached to him. I'd had the horse a couple of years when one evening I was going to Spencerville to leave him in a paddock there next door to a friend's place, but when I arrived my friend wasn't home. So I decided to take him to my friend Joe's place in Turner's Road off Marshlands Road and leave him there overnight. When I arrived, Joe's friend said, "I will put him away for you." This is something I lived to regret. I handed him the reins, and said, "Make sure you shut the gate properly."

Joe was telling me that they had just increased the top prize for the Golden Kiwi Lottery, and my reply was, "If you win it, you might have enough money to buy my horse."

That same night as I left Joe's at ten o'clock we found Little Bull was not in the paddock, so we frantically jumped in Joe's car and went looking for him. We found him just around the corner from Turner's Rd in Marshland Rd. He had been hit by a car driven by a young lady. He had apparently gone right over the top of the car and hit the trailer she was towing. She was very distressed, unhurt and more concerned about the welfare of my horse than any damage to her vehicle. Little Bull had a broken pelvis but was on his feet. He pushed his nose into me and let out a deep sigh. I was overcome with grief. I said to him "What have you done to yourself, you silly old bugger?" We called a vet who came out and euthanized him, and then waited with him until about one a.m. until his body was removed.

I had three other horses after this, but never one that compared with Little Bull and I lost interest after that.

Anyway, at Island Hills the little party of four, Dan, Alan, Joe and myself headed out with our dogs and leading Steel loaded with all our gear. This was great, not having to carry anything. Along the

way, it started to get pretty warm in my red and white nylon jacket. It was one that was reversible, red shower-proof on one side and white brushed-nylon on the other. Taking my jacket off, I stuffed it in under some other gear on the side of the saddle and forgot all about it. We were progressing nicely, until we came upon a fence line, which although heading in the right general direction, was pushing us into some soft ground where we stopped to discuss our next move. The horse had stopped, and refused to budge. None of us had noticed a gate through to the other side. When I looked back, I could not believe my eyes: Steel the horse sinking in the mud, had diminished to the size of a Shetland pony. He reared up, got his front legs over the top wire, then kicked and lunged his way across until he was on the right side of the fence where he lay on his side. We needed to go through the fence to remove the pack-saddle.

Next thing a blood-curdling scream rent the air. A blood-curdling scream with a Dutch accent. "The horse, the horse – its guts has fallen out!" When we looked, my red and white jacket was on the ground beneath the horse's stomach.

We were greatly relieved when we got Steel back on his feet, and found he didn't have a mark on him. Joe the Dutchman took longer

With the horse that jumped the fence, Alan Orchard, the horse Steel, Saki the dog, and me.

to recover from the ordeal than the horse did. A short distance from the valley camp hut there is a small holding paddock where Arthur had told us to leave the horse for the duration of our stay. We hunted morning, noon and night and by the end of our visit we had several pigs and a deer or two, then it came time to pack up and head for home.

As there were no volunteers to go and get the horse, we drew straws and unfortunately Muggins here ended up with the short one. Covered in three days of dried blood and pig and deer smell I cautiously approached Steel with the bridle hidden behind my back, but he didn't want to know me. I could almost read his mind. "There's one of those stupid bastards that led me into the swamp, let them carry their own pigs and deer." And who could blame him? I tried sweet-talking him, I tried ignoring him but in the end he jumped the fence and headed back to the farm leaving us to carry what we could. According to Shand, that fence was the first one Steel had ever jumped in his life.

On the way out we came across a party in a Land Rover. The owner was a local garage proprietor from whom we had previously purchased a well-worn second-hand tyre for our dog trailer. This man and his passengers admired the pigs that we had managed to carry out, and asked if we might sell him one, to which we agreed. The garage owner asked how much, and Dan replied, "Three pounds ten." To which the garage owner said, "That's a bit dear, isn't it?" And Dan said, "No dearer than that bald tyre you sold us." He paid the price!

On every occasion we hunted on Island Hills, the adventures were memorable with no two trips being the same. The winters in the mountains were very cold. And the coldest I have ever felt was when we spent the night out in the open after walking through to the head of Gorge Stream from the Valley Camp.

I had taken a sheet of clear plastic to put under my sleeping bag to keep the dampness at bay. It was so cold the frozen ground stayed white throughout the day. Sleeping for more than two hours at a

TOP: 160 lbs boar which became stuck between the trees.
BOTTOM: Shands, Island Hills 160lbs.

time that first night was an impossibility, and the side of my body touching the ground ached like toothache. I would get back to sleep after rolling on to my other side, only to wake up again after another short fitful sleep. The solution was staring me in the face, but at the time I was too inexperienced to recognize it. The hillside was covered in fern, which makes a good comfy bed and most importantly gets you off the ground. Some of my most comfortable sleeps since have been out on the hills amongst the fern, and on more than one occasion I have seen pigs or deer very close before getting out of my sleeping bag in the mornings.

The walk through to Gorge Stream was through a series of saddles but I don't remember getting on to any pigs on the way through. I think we had left the warmer and better pig country behind, but there was a large mob of deer on a fern-covered face when we arrived. Dan opened up on them with his .222 rifle and at any one time three or four deer would be lying in the fern wounded. However they kept getting up only to be shot again and fell over once more. But they got away. The only deer we ended up with was one that ran down hill into a swampy area where we were and Hutch the dog grabbed it as it tried to run past.

Another memory of the Valley Camp is the basin of water left in front of the fire overnight which froze and had an inch of ice on its surface even though the fire hadn't died out completely.

On a trip to stay at the bush hut, also on Island Hills, I inadvertently left my sleeping bag at home, and hadn't realized this until too late. Luckily the bunks had Kapok mattresses, so I was able to keep warm by sleeping sandwiched between two of them. We always got plenty of pigs, not all of them were monsters, but it was a good place for big sows.

The Bush Hut was, as the name suggests, in the native bush and was made from the available logs by a Norwegian using nothing but an axe. He made a beautiful job of this, but I often wondered if with it being untreated timber it has withstood the ravages of time.

Alan Orchard was another person Dan and I used to regularly go hunting with and he was always very generous with allowing his vehicles to be used, not just his cars, he also bought a Gnat for our use. The Gnat was a three-wheeled vehicle, powered by a five horsepower Honda stationary engine. It was very economical. Our spare fuel was carried in a one-quart oil tin, but I don't know if it was ever needed. The dog-box fitted on to the seats and was capable of being put on the trailer when the Gnat was removed, so the Gnat could tow its own trailer with the dogs in the box if needed. We were the flashiest pig hunters around, as Alan's cars were always the best, Mercedes, late model Fiats, Austin Princess Vanden Plas and so on.

THE HOGGING SOW

Island Hills was one of our very favourite places, and we had some enjoyable times there only marred by losing two of our dogs to poison one weekend. Although the farmer said no poison had been laid for years, it had most likely remained in some old bones that the dogs had scavenged.

Island Hills was beautiful, opening to hilly country surrounded by mountains going from manuka to native bush and wide-open areas of undulating country. Heading out to the valley camp one fine sunny day Alan Orchard, Dan Robin, Neil Pavitt and I had stopped on the way out to see if any game was visible from the track. At the foot of a steep hill where we were, Dan looked through his riflescope and almost immediately discovered a couple of deer hiding in the scrub at the top of the hill. Being fit and keen, I volunteered to go up there. As I climbed higher I could see that the deer had turned into Herefords! Not to worry; I would take the dogs in a big loop before I returned to see if I could get Hutch, Scamp or Saki on to the scent of a boar. I followed a steep-sided creek downhill walking on a flattish area with large patches of exposed red clay showing amongst the scattered scrub. There were few places the creek could be crossed, as the walls were vertical for about twenty feet, so when Hutch and Scamp started bailing a boar on the far side I desperately started searching for a way across. I found a track and was about to go down it when I realised something was on its way up.

Suddenly I stepped back out of the way as a large sow emerged with a snort and a grunt to be confronted by Saki and me. With me yelling, "Get him, get him," Saki latched on to an ear and was

The Hogging Sow and 176lb Boar: Daniel Robin, Fred (surname unknown), and Neil Pavott.

being swung violently around in circles while I tried to grab a leg... If only it would stop spinning.... Eventually I got a hold and stuck the sow as quickly as I could. Meanwhile I had heard Hutch grab the boar, hold for a short while then get thrown off. No pig I had ever seen had done this before, but this pig wasn't going to get away with it either. As Saki and I left the sow, I heard Hutch and Scamp stop the boar further downhill for a second time. I still had not seen the pig. In full flight downhill through the patches of red clay Dan, who unbeknown to me had followed me up the hill, tried to follow the footprints but reckoned he had trouble because he said they were about twenty feet apart. Before I got there the boar broke for the second time and I remember thinking "This one's going to get away, and I am not even going to see it." However with another dog to help hold, that didn't happen, and I soon found them in the steep-sided creek at the bottom of a waterfall.

When I first saw them the boar was lifting both the larger dogs off the ground as he fought to shake them off. He was not a happy chappie at all about having being interrupted in his lovemaking. I had to choose the moment very carefully before jumping into the very confined space with them.

The boar didn't die easily. He was high on adrenalin no doubt, and was a magnificent specimen of the blue-grey pigs found in the North Canterbury foothills. He was big, young, long legged and in his prime. Almost a shame to kill him – almost. By this time Dan had turned up and we started dragging our trophy out when we heard a feminine voice yell out "Yoo-hoo!" We thought it was one of the boys being silly and having us on so replied "Yoo-hoo to you too." A few more paces, and we stepped out into a clearing to be met by a group of tourists on horseback being shown the sights by the farmer's daughter. Everyone was quite impressed and they took many photos.

Sometime in the eighties, Dave Whiting, Shaun Brown and I obtained permission to hunt a small pine block that had been planted about four years previously, and the trees were yet to have a first prune, and as the trees had been planted fairly closely together, the lower branches started at ground level making a nice dense warm sloping face for any pigs who might desire a good home. I had my three dogs Pip, Ricky and Jean and after walking into the pines a short distance I heard the dogs get on to a boar, which broke downhill and tried to outrun them. The boar put on a good sprint but quickly came to a sudden halt. As I got closer I could see he had a problem. His head had passed between the fork in the trunk of a defective tree, which had two main trunks starting from ground level and formed a V shape large enough for the pig's head to pass through, but not his body. So he was stuck with Pip and Jean with an ear each while Ricky had him by the nose. He was going nowhere. It was a simple matter to kill, gut and carry him a short distance downhill to Dave's Land Rover. Close by this area a group of us, including Dan Robin, had been escorted by Arthur Shand on his horse to a vantage point where he pointed out a dense thicket

Daniel and me on the gnat at Shands.

TOP: Stuck, with a broken chain. Daniel and me. BOTTOM LEFT: Me, the dogs and the little boar that chased me around the swamp. RIGHT: Alan Orchard and Daniel carrying a 190lb Boar.

of waste high matagouri. One of his men had been attacked there a couple of weeks previously while out mustering. He wasn't quite sure whether the worker had been ripped or if the knife in his hand had cut him while fighting off the pig, but he had been injured. We had hardly started on our hunt and Arthur had just turned his horse around and headed home when there were a couple of barks, and the boar met his match in Hutch, our champion, the Mohammed Ali of holders. The boar was a battle-scarred old man pig and weighed around one hundred and forty pounds on the hook.

We pig hunters worked harder at our sport than we would ever do for a boss. I have jumped out of bed, driven more than one hundred and thirty kilometres to Waipara, round trip, gone hunting, got pigs, and still been able to get to get back to my job as a roofer and working on a roof by eight a.m. Or, during the roar, at Oxford, I've slept out on the hills amongst the roots of large trees while a storm raged and the wind howled through the branches which carried the rain away from my downwind bed where I lay in my sleeping bag with its waterproof cover. I would still be early for work after a sixty kilometre drive back to Christchurch.

OPPOSITE: Me helping Daniel get a pig on his back.
TOP: Valley Camp Hut, now demolished. BOTTOM: Now, get up Daniel!

TOP: Sandy the dog (right of photo) grabs a boar in the manuka, I am ready with bayonet. BOTTOM: Saki the dog, me and Alan. OPPOSITE: Alan Orchard and pig.

My, what big teeth you have!

CHAPTER 9

Hunting on Forestry Land

A LOT OF GOOD BOARS have come out of Ashley Forest. It's not so easy to obtain permits these days unless you belong to a pig hunting club. Even when permits were not too hard to get I seldom hunted the Ashley, mainly because of the amount of gorse growing there and my own experience of such conditions. Later on I came to like the forest when I wore canvas leggings over my shorts and leather gloves, and found that if you were quick you could be the first to drive around the boundary of your block with a dog, or dogs on the bonnet of the vehicle or on top of the dog-box to pick up any fresh scents or sign.

Usually, when Des Campbell and I teamed up we would stop the car where the dogs looked most interested, then split up and walk in opposite directions on the road for a while to make sure we weren't missing anything, and then would get back together again.

On one such hunt we had been apart for about twenty minutes and I hadn't seen my dogs for the majority of that time, so went

Me on the left, unknown person in the middle and Des Campbell on the right, with our dogs.

back to meet with Des. The first thing he said was, "Your dogs have got a boar down there." He was pointing to a face covered in gorse which was well above my head. There was no noise at all, just the buzz of the bees and other insects and it was a beautiful still warm day. Suddenly the dogs started barking for a short while, followed by silence apart from some heavy breathing, but no squeals, so I knew immediately that they had a good one. Normally a big tough pig does not squeal.

I cursed as I struggled to make any headway through the gorse, sometimes walking on top and sometimes slipping down to waist height, always conscious of the danger of my dogs being injured. I hurried down to where I stood on top of where they were all wedged tightly in the gorse beneath. All I could do was to part the matted gorse then slide face-first into the hole and try to stick the boar, but this was difficult because there was a dog wedged tightly on either side of the boar. The hole I had made to get at him took me straight down on to the pig's back, but the dogs were in the way of me being able to stick it. As I put my hand on the pig's back the boar dragged the dogs forward allowing me to finally get a hold of one back leg. After he was killed and gutted Des came down and between us we dragged the carcass one pull at a time up the fifty yards to the car. He was a good forestry boar with a really nice set of tusks. At the time, a guy who came to our club was doing a study of the pigs caught in the forest, and he was able to tell the ages of the pigs within a month, by the markings of the ring marks on the teeth, just like you can with a tree, and he told us that this pig was three and a half years old. He weighed 160lbs.

Once, on another hunt, my dog Bee was in the bottom of a gully and disturbed a large boar. I went part of the way down a ridge which was at ninety degrees to the road and stopped halfway down in thick broom, gorse and young trees, when I realised that the boar was coming uphill no more than fifty feet away. As he moved I also moved, thinking that if we arrived on the roadside together I may be able to get a shot at him.

However, with the amazing sense of smell that a pig has, he stopped, raised his head and sniffed the air, making a sound like air being drawn into a forty-four gallon drum. I could not see this happening, but could envisage it – the noise the pig made was so loud. He realized that if he moved, I would move too, keeping pace with him. Next minute he turned, and went straight back downhill crashing his way through the undergrowth like a bulldozer, and got away. Lucky Pig!

Another time I was there, in the heart of the forest, with a friend Nelson North, and we were without a firearm. We were well off the road with my two dogs, Ricky and Spook. I came upon a wet gully with fresh big boar sign. The dogs were very keen and raced ahead. I still hadn't entered the gully when I heard them bailing in the distance, then after a short time it went quiet and I realized the big boar had broken free. I heard him crashing up towards me through the trees. I was standing on a damp well-worn pig track through thick fern and pine trees on my side of the gully. I decided to press myself into the fern, and if the pig kept on the track I was on, I would make a lunge for his heart with my bayonet as he rushed by. However, the moment he appeared opposite me, he put on the brakes, stopped, sniffed the air, and thundered downhill smashing his way through the centre of the gully and was gone to live another day.

On another Ashley hunt with my dogs Bee, Bonnie, and Karl, a Great Dane cross, I thought I would walk inside the pine plantation which had grown enough to suppress most of the gorse. The morning was frosty and I wore several layers of clothing with the old army coat on the outside keeping me nice and warm. The dogs were keen and had beaten me out of the small gully I was in, to a ridge ahead where, as I arrived, I could hear them bailing strongly deep down in the other side. Although there were plenty of trees where I was, the gorse began to get thicker as I descended, so I decided my best approach would be to walk along the ridge until I was directly above them as it is a lot harder to sidle in the thick stuff. It is usually a lot easier to come straight down. I had my gun under my coat, so was completely unprepared when two large boars came rushing up the hill towards me. They didn't change course. I could only walk backwards while being eye to eye with the closer of the two as they passed by within a few feet and crashed down the hill on the other side, back the way I had just come.

Luckily for me, the dogs and their boar had moved to a different position, further down the ridge I was on, and I could hear some unfamiliar dogs barking, so guessed they belonged to the boys on the adjoining hunting block. My guess was right, and the dogs were getting a beating from the pig. As I worked my way down towards them the noise gradually tapered off until there was only one dog barking; my dog Bee.

Getting closer I found several strange dogs lying injured. The boar was under the gorse and looking at me from about six feet when I shot him. He went straight down. I thought he was standing side on when I pulled the trigger, but I was wrong, because later when he was skinned we found the bullet had entered from the front shoulder area, travelled the length of the body and lodged just under the skin on the opposite side back leg, meaning he must have been facing me. The owners of the injured dogs came over and helped by carrying the pig up the hill for us. They were young and fit – I wasn't. I was very grateful for their help. If I remember correctly this pig was another 160lb boar.

Hunting the Ashley Forest is not as freely available now. For the last twenty-five years or more the average private hunter has generally had access to forestry land denied, but the pig hunting clubs are able to go there due to the fact that the clubs carry insurance and are more organized.

Club hunts are a good way to keep pig numbers down because with so many men and different packs of dogs, the pigs do get a hard time, never knowing if they are going to run into a fresh pack of hunters. Just sitting eating your lunch can be very productive at times with pigs running up or crossing the road nearby.

On this occasion with Des Campbell we were each driving our own vehicles but met up for a chat. While we were talking Des, who had a walkie-talkie, received a call from his friend Mark Hookham who was on a road well above us and we arranged to meet up for lunch. I followed Des in my vehicle until we came to a T-intersection where Des turned left when he should have gone to his right, so I overtook him by turning right when he had to stop and retrace his route. The forestry road twisted and turned through the trees until I came upon a piece of straight road about one hundred and fifty metres long where I encountered a good-sized black pig running straight towards me. Quickly braking and pulling up sideways across the road I put my old .303 out the driver's side window, shot it dead. I then drove to where it lay quivering on the roadside. Des arrived as I pulled up at the pig and said, "Don't touch it" When I asked why, he said, "It might have been poisoned."

"It has," I agreed, " – lead poisoning!"

Everything had happened so quickly that Des hadn't seen or heard anything until he saw me standing by the quivering pig, which had just escaped from some dogs.

Another time Des and I were in separate vehicles on a forestry road overlooking the Selwyn River. Des was looking through his binoculars across the scrub-covered side we were on to the adjoining grassy farmland when he noticed a black sow of about one hundred and thirty pounds running towards the river below us. Des wanted to let the dogs out, but I managed to talk him out of

Des Campbell with our 160lb Ashley Forest Boar. (good tusks)

that, as we were about fifty metres back from a sheer cliff, which dropped off into the riverbed. The dogs could not have got down into it. Between the road and the cliff top was scrubby manuka about seven or eight feet tall. The pig disappeared on to the riverbed as I grabbed the .303 and sneaked down to the cliff edge where at first I could see nothing. Then I saw four sheep standing in the riverbed staring in one direction. Following their gaze, I spotted a nice black sow drinking at the water's edge. It wasn't an easy shot, as I had to stand on my tiptoes to even see it, so I was quite pleased when I pulled the trigger: the pig jumped in the air and collapsed in a spray of water, and the pig lay dead. Without driving too far we found a track down on to the riverbed, and we drove to right where it lay. The pig had escaped someone else's dogs (its ears were bleeding) only to have the misfortune to run into us.

JOLLYBROOK

Many years ago the only hunting available to a lot of hunters was either forestry blocks or Department of Conservation land. Sometimes you had to go into a ballot which was drawn on a certain day of the week. If you were lucky enough to be chosen, the onus was on the hunter to pick up the permit from a pre-determined pickup point prior to the weekend.

Other areas, like the Jollybrook, were a bit easier, with more than one permit issued for the same day, so it was a good idea to get an early start to avoid congestion.

Colin Hurrell was a long-time acquaintance who had no dogs but liked to go for a walk occasionally, and when he told me he had seen fresh pig rooting up a creek near Lake Sumner, I said I would bring the dogs up there providing he got permission, which he did. We nearly froze to death in Colin's SWB canvas-top Land Rover and the so-called heater was useless. The minute we started up the creek the dogs were keen and we knew it wouldn't be long before the dogs had a pig. The creek was full of twists and turns and the dogs were racing ahead. Colin and I were going as fast as we could, but were getting left behind.

After around about half a dozen bends, we came upon the dogs with a nice fat eating sow, so didn't bother going any further as we had all we needed.

Colin became enthusiastic, and so we obtained a permit for the Jollybrook once more and travelled there in his Land Rover in mid-winter, with heavy frost and snow on the tops. It was really cold. Upon arriving at the Jollybrook swing-bridge we were a bit disappointed to discover another vehicle parked, and the occupants well gone. Obviously we would be walking in behind them. This is not always a bad thing as the dogs could be an equaliser if the other party only had rifles. I had Saki and Dinda and Patch, the old spayed pointer-cross, which I later sold to Colin. She was a good old dog and had been a great help with the training of my pups. I had found her from an ad in the paper one Saturday morning. The owner was giving up hunting and she was his finder.

We hadn't gone further than three quarters of a mile when Dinda started to bark, and I knew straight away by the sound of it he was bailing a deer. I told Colin not to waste his time trying to get there, as it would be gone in a minute. Dinda used to bail deer for a short period, but was too slow to catch them when they ran. They were in a thick patch of manuka about two hundred yards above us. Then as time went by I knew the other dogs had arrived and the deer was being held, so I hurried up the hill and put it out of its misery.

Upon inspection, I found that the deer, a yearling, had been shot that morning, and had a broken leg so we had done it a favour, rather than it being left to die slowly. Luckily the deer didn't weigh much, but a couple of hundred yards from the swing-bridge there was a ford, so I suggested that we walk across and drive down and then pick up the animal, but Colin would have none of it. No way did he want to cross the freezing river and get wet.

By this time Colin had walked off and left me, so I started off across the river where I found it swifter and deeper than I thought. By the time I reached the halfway point, I was starting to have second thoughts about my decision, as I was having trouble keeping my footing and the rocks beneath were very slippery. I hesitated, then turned around to make up my mind whether to continue or go back, when suddenly I found myself floating face-first down the Hurunui River. The deer on my back was filling with water and holding me under, as I had tied the deer's legs in the form of a pack. So I quickly put my arms above my head and slipped out of it, grabbing a leg to stop it being swept away down the river, and lunged and plunged and dragged the deer on to a shingle bank, which was about twelve feet from the far side. When I had a look the water was deep, and coloured blue-green in the next channel. I walked upstream as far as was necessary to cross the final stretch. I ended up taking my clothes off because I didn't have any spare gear, so the wet stuff was wrung out and had to be put back on. I nearly froze to death!

I sold my dog Patch to Colin, but I don't believe he ever took her out. Six months later she had doubled in weight, and she was obviously not being exercised enough. She was lucky though, because somehow she ended up with Neville Stokes, a keen hunter.

Early one morning while driving up the Lake Sumner Road to the Jollybrook, I was in my old Mark 2 Consul with only one headlight working, and was driving slowly along the rough road in pitch-black darkness when I realized an animal was running beside the car and casting a shadow on the roadside because it was so close to the front of the car. For one moment I thought "possum", then realized it was too big. It was a pig of about fifty pounds.

I skidded to a stop and let Dinda and Saki out of the boot. The pig meanwhile had doubled back and started up the bank on the high side of the road; without dogs to follow the scent in the dark it would have escaped. Anyway I accepted this gift, and thought, "What a great start to the day." But I was to be disappointed. I parked by the Jollybrook swing-bridge, and spent the rest of the day walking the hills without getting on to or seeing any more animals.

Hunting at Jollybrook.

CHAPTER 10

Old Jack Barker

JACK BARKER WAS WELL KNOWN. As an ex-publican, and a man who lived to hunt. He had many friends, and loved the company of younger people whose company he claimed help keep him young. He had a kindly weather-beaten face and we always knew him as Old Jack. He was one of those people you couldn't imagine any other way. Jack was only fifty-six when he died, but to us young hunters he always looked an old man.

I first ran across Jack when my friend Ray from Kaikoura arranged a trip into the "Stag and Spey", a farm on the inland road to Kaikoura. Ray had two good dogs and I had four. We knew that Jack had recently been in hospital, and Ray seemed to think he wouldn't have any dogs, although he did have two prior to being hospitalised for a crook heart. Supposedly he had angina, and carried pills to take whenever he had any chest pains. Jack loved company, the more the merrier so far as he was concerned, so it was only with slight surprise that when we arrived at the old house we were staying in we found Jack had borrowed a couple of dogs from a friend, and also invited Barry who had six dogs, one of which was a bitch in season. Fourteen dogs in total! This should have meant a massive cleanout of pigs. Sorry, it doesn't work that way! We had collie crosses, bulldog crosses, Great Dane crosses, foxy-crosses and just about any other breed you could think of – all interested in Barry's bitch! We got a few pigs that weekend, but we spent a good deal of our time keeping the dogs apart. This put a dampener on the whole trip.

As the weekend drew to a close, Jack suggested that I stay on an extra day in Kaikoura, instead of going back to Christchurch. The incentive was that that he would take me to a sure-fire place to get a boar to help pay for my missed day's wages. Jack explained that all the local hunters knew of this place, but didn't have the dogs to stop the pigs, so they had more or less given up on this patch which was just about vertical and covered in thick scrub, large trees and, worst of all, very big old man stinging nettle.

At that time I shared dogs with my good friend Diesel Dan, and one of them was the best holder I have ever seen. He was named Hutch, sometimes called Chuck; his mother was a pure-bred British bulldog, and his father a Labrador. He was without a doubt the Mohammed Ali of pig dogs. I have watched him with big boars bailing inches from their nose, his head bobbing and weaving, side to side, up and down, until at last he would make his move and grab an ear. I have been him being thrown around four feet in the air with his legs splaying out like a cat. He always managed to keep out of the way of the tusks, loved holding big boars, but was never ripped.

Another of the dogs, Dinda, was out of a golden cocker spaniel, by an Airedale bull terrier-cross father. He was black, as was Hutch, with a nuggetty body, a whiskery face and wiry coat, but spaniel size. He was a very good finder and would hold also. The third dog Saki, was out of a collie bitch and Hutch was the father. The fourth dog Scamp was a foxy-cross. They could all find and hold, so it didn't take long for them to get on to a boar, which promptly bolted to the bottom of a gully where the stinging nettles were at their thickest. This pig, although not big (one hundred and thirty pounds) had a good even jaw and was all that I wanted to carry out of this almost vertical country. Jack couldn't help, and I never expected any from a man in his condition. That afternoon I returned to Christchurch, selling the pig to game-buyers Logan Brothers at Waikari on the way home. That evening I received a call from Dan. He had arranged a hunt for the following day to Waiau, and the dogs could hardly walk. I warned him that they might not be as energetic as normal, but he and Alan still came home with a nice big sow, and the dogs to a well-earned rest.

Jack had a habit of putting his boots on before anyone else, grabbing his old rifle with a quarter-inch nut as an aperture sight, getting his two dogs, Flynn, an Airedale-cross and Sam, a bull terrier Labrador-cross, and bolting off at top speed. Given a start, he would take some catching. He was fitter than he looked, and as it transpired, his heart was not his problem. On a weekend away Jack arrived with this great new product called Complan, the complete food according to him. "You don't need anything else," he said. I had carrots, potatoes, cabbage and a fore-quarter of roast mutton, which in those days could be bought for fifty cents from the Canterbury Frozen Meats factory shop on the corner of Main North and Belfast Roads. I would roast the meat the night before and carry it in a big old biscuit tin which had a tight fitting lid and kept out any flies. There was plenty of meat for us, and the dogs, and it didn't take Jack long to go right off Complan which didn't satisfy a hungry hunter like he thought it would. Luckily there was enough meat and veg for everyone, but Jack never turned up again with just a tin of Complan.

Jack and I were out hunting together when a big boar killed my little spaniel-cross Dinda. Back then rip collars and tracking collars were unheard of, and as little Dinda my spaniel-cross grew older, he thought he was indestructible. We hunted most weekends, and two weekends before his demise, Jack and I had gone to a farm near Amberley. The weather was not that good with a gale-force nor-westerly blowing and very hot. Jack's dog Sam was a very good finder, but was inclined to let boars go free as he couldn't always hold them, and came off them without attempting to bail them. So it was this day as we pushed our way through thick waist-high matagouri that I heard the sound of a yelp carried faintly on the wind, then Sam appeared with a couple of fresh pokes in his neck. By this time Dinda and Saki were bailing steadily with their heads pushed into the thick matagouri, which was interlaced with lawyer. I had my .22 ready and was standing right there with the dogs when it had a go at them, ripping Dinda's skin on his throat from the larynx, most of the way to his ear. The boar then bolted straight down the steep-sided gully, bounding like a deer over the top of the prickles. I watched as he beat the dogs to the bottom by a mile, then floundered across a freshly ploughed paddock until he disappeared. He was very impressive, a very thick shield on his shoulders hanging nearly to the ground giving him the appearance of having little short legs. He was an old blue boar who would have seen a lot of dogs off during his lifetime, and he had once more survived a very close call. I had been within six feet of him, but couldn't shoot because I couldn't see him. I took Dinda to the vet, and he was stitched up and was just healing nicely when the next hunt took his life

A couple of weeks later while hunting on Glen Colwyn farm, which is on the way to Kaikoura, Jack and I climbed to the top of the hill overlooking Conway Flats. On the way up we climbed a spur, which overlooked a large bush valley. Halfway up the dogs got on to a stag which gave the dogs a good run around before finally making his escape. We continued on and were part of the way down the hill on the sea side. We had a good long day and we were returning to my car (a 1947 V8) the same way past the bush valley when the dogs began to bail deep inside the valley, but below us. As I went to overtake Jack he offered me his .303, thinking that the dogs had bailed the stag which he had seen earlier in the day, but I turned it down as Saki was bailing, and he only barked on pigs. When I reached the scene I found Saki and Dinda had a nice black boar backed into some tall-head tussocks.

I was on a two-foot ledge behind my dogs, looking slightly down on top of them. I took my .22 out and fired one shot and the rifle jammed. Saki, expecting the pig to go down flew in, front on to grab the pig's right ear. I can still see Dinda in mid-air as he jumped to grab the other ear, but he never made it. The pig lashed out and caught poor Dinda in the throat where he had the stitches from the Amberley boar. The pig then broke with the dogs in hot pursuit.

By this time it was almost dark as I walked around trying to locate the dogs but without success. We had only come hunting for the day from Christchurch, but ended up sleeping in the car for the night because the dogs were still missing. Scamp the foxy-cross arrived back at the car at three a.m. Saki was found on the hill about seven a.m. not far from where I saw him last and none the worst for his night out. But Dinda was never seen again. I advertised in *The Press*, but without luck. I believe the pig had hit him in the neck, and in the excitement he took off after it without realizing he was mortally injured, only to die when he ran out of blood.

I could have done things differently, maybe I should have taken Jack's rifle; this particular .22 was known to jam sometimes. I always tried to fire two quick shots and nearly every time the animal I was shooting at would go straight down, mainly because the animals were so close. Losing Dinda was a blow as we all get very attached to our dogs and I really liked that wee fellow.

One beautiful fine sunny day without a cloud in the sky Jack Barker and I were climbing a steep ferny hill above Conway Flats. We decided to go up to a bush-covered ridge that we could see above us in the distance. As we came up over the ridge we found we were looking into a large ferny basin facing east; it would be warm all year round. As soon as we looked, the dogs were chasing a large mob of deer, up to twelve in number, which disappeared all except for one hind which stood about one hundred yards away at the edge of the bush staring back at us. Jack carried an ancient .303 rifle, which had a quarter-inch nut welded to it for a back sight, and he quickly brought this up to his shoulder, and fired. The hind never flinched. Three or four more shots, and still she stood there. Maybe she had heard about Jack's shooting and felt safe. Anyway, Jack refused to fire again claiming that she deserved to live, and put his rifle away.

It was then that I told him that when he fired the first shot I saw the fern in the basin move, so we guessed there was a pig in here. We had quite a long wait before we got some dogs back, so I could take them through the area. What had looked to be about a metre high was above my head, and ancient logs up to four feet thick lay throughout.

I started out and the dogs went ahead keenly, while Jack stayed and oversaw proceedings. I had arrived around the middle of the basin when Jack yelled, "The pig has come out on the other side."

"How big is it?" I asked. He said it was about a hundred pounds, and asked me if I wanted him to shoot it. Having witnessed his shooting, I didn't want him chasing the pig away any faster than it was already moving, so I politely refused.

When I arrived at where Jack last saw the pig, there was no sign of it, or the dogs. All was quiet, no wind, bright blue sky, and hardly a ripple on the ocean. Then, two ridges away, galloping like a horse, I saw this impressive large black boar, the dogs strung out in single file behind. At first it was always at least a bend ahead, but when at last they saw it, the speed went on. They caught up right on a sharp bend, where they hit him and spun him around. I knew I had to get there as fast as possible, but made a stupid mistake by taking the most direct route which took me steeper and steeper towards a creek with a waterfall.

I had no choice but to retrace my steps, until I went around the heads of the gullies to come down the correct spur. As I ran to the point on the track where I last saw them I found where the surface of the track had been scuffed up. All was silent for a moment until I looked over the edge where the fern had been flattened, and saw the dogs and the pig with his backside sticking out of the fern. One dog had an ear while lying on his back on the ground with his four feet in the air, and the others lay around panting. It was a very hot day. The dogs and the pig were all stuffed, so it was an easy matter to go down and kill the boar with the bayonet.

By the time I had the pig gutted, Jack had arrived. The way out of this small flat area just above a creek was almost straight up, and Jack couldn't help, so it was slow and sure with plenty of rests to reach the track above, which led back to the car.

I took the pig back to Christchurch to show my friends before selling him to the game-buyers next day. He weighed two hundred and twenty-four pounds on the hook (102kg).

The 224lb hog at Conway Flats.

TOP: Waiau Large boar; 180 lbs with Daniel's children Mark and Lisa.
BOTTOM: Barry, Jack and Ray with thirteen male dogs and one bitch in season!

TOP: Barry Watson, Jack Barker in the middle, and Ray Thompson on the right.
BOTTOM: At the Blue Duck, Kaikoura: A nice even jaw. This pig paid my day's wages.

CHAPTER 11

Tame Wild Pigs

A LOT OF HUNTERS ARE tempted into bringing young pigs home, either as pets or to fatten up or with the idea of releasing them later. When you live in a city this can cause numerous problems unforeseen by these hunters until the neighbours complain, not to you but to the local council which of course has rules about that sort of thing, and will quickly have a letter in the post, along with a copy of the relevant bylaws.

I suppose I was lucky to get a black sow from piglet to one hundred and twenty pounds live weight in eight months. I weighed it by putting some food on the ground, and as it went to eat, I quickly put my arms under and around its stomach and then whipped it up off the ground before it could run away. Then it was on to the bathroom scales, and I subtracted my own weight from the total to get the sow's weight. The pig was exceptionally clean, as all pigs are if given the opportunity, only doing its business in one corner of the section. It lived with my dogs and they understood this was my pet pig and never attempted to harm it. As a matter of fact I reckon I could have taken it hunting with the dogs.

It used to make little squeaking noises while gently chewing affectionately on the fingers of my hand and fluttering its beautiful long black eyelashes. I was a sucker for this pig and could never have killed or eaten it. Dan was around one day when I said "Put your fingers in its mouth, it won't bite," but Dan replied, "Like hell, it would probably bite my fingers off," and he could have been right.

One morning shortly after I woke, I looked out the kitchen window and did a double-take. The surface of my back lawn was completely gone, and resembled a freshly ploughed paddock. The pig had escaped from the enclosed area at the rear of my section. Thank God it had not gone off down the street and destroyed the neighbour's properties as well. Reluctantly, I realized that time had run out for this sow and it would have to go.

I found a buyer that had no sentimental attachment to my pig, and had no qualms about killing it. He left a high-sided trailer the night before I was due to go hunting so I could put the pig in before I departed. I sold the pig to this person only after making him promise it wouldn't feel anything and it would be killed humanely. He told me later it was the best pig he ever bought and killed, because it wasn't overly fat, and had beautiful sweet juicy flesh. I had always fed it on the best tucker like potatoes, tomatoes or any leftover food from the household, and from friends' households and it had been well fed.

To make sure I wasn't caught out again the next two piglets I brought home were left at my friend George's place on the other side of town where, luckily, the neighbours must have been tolerant as no complaints were ever received before they grew to seventy pounds and I removed them. The pigs were both silver-grey sows and came from Waiau where that colour for pigs is common.

It was Christmas 1971 when Peter Robin, who was Diesel Dan's younger brother, and I put the two pigs in a trailer to add some fresh genes to the pigs at Murchison, the object being that we would later find bigger and better pigs. The last we saw of them they were trotting off up our friend's farm track stopping every now and again to poke around in the mud. They seemed to be very happy to be released.

I had kept in touch with my friends at Murchison by mail, so learned a few months later that a local hunter's dog had caught one of the sows that we had released earlier and she was heavily pregnant when they killed her. The other sow was never seen again by anyone we knew, and a few months later a helicopter pilot told my friends he had seen a good mob of pigs at the back of their property, and they were mainly grey in colour, so it seems that at least one of my sows survived long enough to have at least one litter.

A friend, Charley Baker, took a little grey boar home from Waiau, and this pig was scared of nothing. If you pushed him gently away with your feet, he would rush back at you, mouth wide open and would try to bite. This was quite comical as Charley let him in the kitchen on the linoleum floor and the poor little bugger had trouble getting a grip on it, causing major wheel-spin or leg-spin in this case when he tried to rush at you.

Glyn Wye had a game park at that time, and as was inevitable the little pig became too big and stroppy for town, so ended up in the Glyn Wye Park, where he ran a tusk up the leg of a person feeding him. After that I lost track of him. It is quite possible he was put down before he did some real damage. I knew of at least one person who had been killed by a boar, and at least two others who had been scarred for life. So it pays not to treat them too lightly, but to be cautious around them at all times and treat them with respect. Trust nothing with balls, man or beast.

Arthur Shand had a large grey sow he called Lucy, which I would estimate weighed around five hundred pounds (227kg) or more, live weight. Some hunters from Hamner shot her not far from Shand's house. They obviously didn't know she was a pet, but it put the brakes on the hunting for a while, as Arthur and his wife were quite fond of this sow and used to take her around the schools to show the children.

Another friend kept a young boar from Ashley Forest until it became a monster and lived in town for several years. On one side of his jaw his tusks protruded six and seven eighths of an inch, and the tip was broken off. On the other side seven and one-quarter inches of tusk protruded. I had this head mounted by taxidermist Peter Ritchie from Christchurch who did a first-class job. (Some mounted heads I have seen are pathetic, and just don't look right, because they don't show the bulk of a pig's neck) Peter was also a hunting and fishing guide and owned a golden Labrador. As he regularly took it out of town into other areas, he had to carry a certificate with him to prove it had been treated for Hydatids within the previous six weeks. I was working for the council and would visit him every six weeks to dose his dog, and asked him what it would cost to mount a pig's head for me. He gave me a price and it was a good one so far as I was concerned, but as I walked up his drive carrying the head, Peter's first words when he saw it were, "Bloody hell, that's not a *pig* – oh well, I have given you a price, so I will stick to it!" He suggested that upon mounting he could pull the tusks out even further, but I asked for them to be left as they were, because anyone who had done any pig hunting would easily be able to tell if they had been pulled out of the jaw, and I wanted the mounted boar's head to look genuine.

I had shot this particular pig because he had grown too big to keep in town. I didn't weigh the head or the guts, but minus these two major parts, the carcass tipped the scales at three hundred and sixty-five pounds, which if you take the head and the guts as roughly one third of his total weight, would have made his live weight around five hundred and fifty pounds (250kg). This is how large a tame wild pig can grow if given good tucker and no exercise.

Pigs vary greatly in size in different parts of New Zealand. A friend, who lived near Picton and has a great collection of boar's jaws, told me that many of them were mature pigs weighing no more than fifty-five pounds. However, in the Ashley Forest a lot of pigs weigh two hundred pounds or more.

TAME WILD PIGS

This pig came from Ashley Forest as a piglet. This shows how large a wild boar could possibly grow. The Taxidermist suggested he draw out the tusks, but I insisted they stayed in their natural place. Six and seven eighths inches on one side, and seven and a quarter inches on the other. The carcass, minus the head and gut, weighed 368 lbs.

TOP: Arthur Shand's tame wild sow,"Lucy".
BOTTOM: This tame pig grew to 120 lbs live weight in eight months.

CHAPTER 12

Other Hunts and More Interesting Characters

ERNIE DRAKE WAS THE BARMAN at the Royal George Hotel in Fitzgerald Avenue, commonly known as "The Pig Hunter's Arms" where we gathered for a jug or two on a Thursday after work. It was a real mix of races with Maori, Islanders, Pakeha and the Indians who sold roasted cashews and peanuts. They were delicious, still warm from the roasting and if you preferred, hot ones with a dash of chilli added. This went well with a cold beer and encouraged the amount of alcohol consumption. It was in the days of the six o'clock swill when men would buy jugs of beer two at a time just before closing and then be given till six-thirty to drink it.

The more beer consumed the more outrageous the stories became. For example I had been out with Ernie and we had killed a heavily pregnant sow and as it was cut open he counted the piglets in the total. Ernie said, "They are still pigs, aren't they?"

Ernie was extremely sociable and would invite everyone from the bar to his home barbecues and sometimes had around fifty guests where, dressed in a chef's apron, Ernie would take charge of the cooking. As a duck and swan shooter, they, along with rabbit, hare, pork or venison could all be on the menu. They were great times.

One pig-hunting trip nearly ended in disaster when Ernie, his fourteen-year-old son Wayne and I did a day trip to Boyle Point. To get to the hunting area the river must first be crossed to reach the terraces below the scrub-covered faces, which turned to heavy bush higher up. The day was slightly cloudy, but calm and not too cold, ideal for hunting. The Ministry of Works engineers' camp was close by, so I felt sure they would have had a few hunters there keeping an eye out for handy game. We arrived at daybreak, crossed the river, which was just above our knees at the deepest point, and hunted heading towards the west further into the mountains. After a couple of hours we already had a good eating pig, and decided to head back to the car as it was starting to spit with rain. We noticed that the river had risen considerably, obviously it had been raining heavily further upstream. I stepped off the riverbank, and was up to my waist immediately so went looking for a shallower place to cross.

Ernie had decided that he would carry the pig. This was against my better judgment, because he was older, and I should have carried it being younger and fitter. While they waited and watched from the riverbank, I started to cross just above some rapids where the river was at its widest and took a slight bend to the right looking downstream. The river at this point was now very wide, and I knew by the time I was three-quarters of the way across that I would appear to be nearly at the far bank to them, so I yelled out it was ok, and went back to assist Ernie and Wayne to cross. What I had failed to mention was that the water was so swift between the three-quarter point and the far bank of the river bed, the boulders on the river bed were rolling and could plainly be heard above the roar of the water.

We linked arms, with Wayne in the middle, Ernie and the pig

downstream and me on the topside. When we arrived at this three-quarter point, Ernie was starting to panic and fell face down in the water. I dragged him straight back to his feet while I kept telling him to go downstream, He was arguing that the deerstalkers manual says you have to go upstream. This was ridiculous because it was impossible; our feet were being swept from under us. All of us were having difficulty keeping our footing, and when Ernie went facedown for a second time he came up spouting like a whale. He gave in, and the three of us kicked our way across letting the current carry us. The bend in the river was helpful also. Several times after this Ernie would say to me, "You saved my life you know!"

I am not blowing my own trumpet, just pointing out that panic can be your worst enemy because logic can go out the window. Ernie often showed his appreciation with the odd jug or two.

HUNTING MT WHITE

Bryant Handiside, who was a good keen man and ex-shearer friend of mine, first introduced me to Laurie Bee. Laurie lived at Timaru and had spent a couple of seasons Possuming (killing Possums for their skins) up at Mt White, during which time he had seen pig rooting, but never actually saw a pig. So it was arranged that I would bring my dogs along to track them down.

I had Ricky the staghound spaniel-cross, and Spook my bulldog-cross. The large open tussock country and river terraces suited my dogs to a tee as Rick was a tireless tracker, could cover the vast amounts of country once he got on to a scent and was easy to see due to his liver and white colour. Laurie drove up from Timaru to pick us up in his flash new Land Cruiser, a diesel, which ran so quietly and smoothly I assumed it ran on petrol and was very surprised when I later learned that it was diesel. All the diesels I had ever been associated with up to that time had been clunkers: stinking of fuel and so noisy they would give you a headache if you were in them for any length of time. As I only had two dogs, Bryant decided he would borrow John Roberts' three dogs.

So we set out early one morning with our cut lunches, flasks, and a trailer load of dogs. The weather forecast was for Nor-Westers, strong to gale-force, which usually ruins your day's hunting by bringing rain to the mountains and changing to gusty hot winds by the time they reach the coast. In other words the Canterbury nor-west wind was bad news wherever you hunted. So as we headed down the Old West Coast Road into a strong north-west wind, we were discussing whether or not to continue, when we were buffeted by particularly strong gusts and a few drops of rain and decided to pull over to the roadside for a talk about what we should do. I suggested that as we had come so far, we might as well continue, which we did, to arrive at the Mt White homestead in pouring rain.

The manager advised that we would be unable to get to the pre-arranged hunting area as the creeks and rivers were all in flood, but told us that a couple of weeks previously he had noticed a little bit of rooting beside one of his tracks not too far distant from the house. My first thought was, "Oh yeah, no trouble to find old pig sign – it's not looking good." So as we pulled up at the old sign with a negative attitude I suggested I take my dogs further along the terraced face before I walked up to the next level, while they would go straight up the hill from the vehicle.

There was a break in the weather and the rain had stopped. As I climbed the hill the dogs raced ahead and disappeared over the top, then suddenly I could hear a faint squeal, like a small pig. When I reached the top the noise increased in volume, and I found the dogs had a nice hundred-pound sow which was quickly dispatched and the dogs sent away. The sow had been stopped in a patch of scrubby manuka and the hill above had similar patches of vegetation on it, including matagouri.

While I gutted the first pig, the dogs started to bail fifty metres above me up the hill. When I stood up I saw my dog Ricky get tossed up above the scrub and the pig took off heading downhill straight towards me, only stopping when Spook grabbed it almost in the same spot as its mate lay dead, a nice little hundred pound boar this time.

Shortly afterwards, Laurie and Brian's dogs arrived, so putting on a serious face and trying to be a bit of a smart-ass I said, "OK, we can go home now," amidst vocal protests from the boys. "We've only just got here and we haven't walked any further than a couple of hundred metres." I said, "Alright, we will get one more so we have got one each."

We then sidled around the hill till we came to a spur overlooking a wide gully. It was then I noticed Ricky on the far side with his nose down going in circles trying to pick up a pig scent. To complicate matters a large hare was hopping around in front of him, but he soon found the trail he was looking for and was flat out up a steep hill heading for the top where there was a thick patch of matagouri. This was a sure thing, so I was already on my way over there before the barking started. We did get our third pig after all which was another black one and of similar size to the others. I reckon they were littermates.

The rain had held off all this time and we had just taken some photos, put the dogs in the trailer, and climbed into the back of the cruiser with our food and hot drinks, when the sky opened up and the rain bucketed down. It was such a good feeling to be cozy and warm while listening to the rain and we were so glad we hadn't turned back.

GAINING EXPERIENCE

Many years ago I received a call one evening from a keen young hunter, Richard Brons. He was only about 16 years old at the time, and had a couple of young dogs, and permission to hunt a property at Waiau. He had been referred to me by a mutual friend who told him that I would likely be willing to go out hunting with him to help train his dogs. I picked him up in my 1947 V8 and we drove up to Waiau where we parked on the side of the road and started walking uphill all the way to a back hut about five miles distant. We killed a small pig, about 50 pounds on the way, but didn't see any others. Richard had plenty of questions. One was "Do the pigs go you?" I will always remember my reply with a laugh "No, they only want to get away," little realising that later if I was asked a question like that again I would have to change my story!

After a hard walk we arrived at the back hut, had a quick look around, and after short break started off again through some dense manuka. We hadn't walked far at all when my two dogs Sooty and Nero bailed a nice black boar. When I saw the pig I thought to myself that he's not a bad specimen. He was about a hundred and sixty pounds with a good jaw. I was standing directly behind my two dogs and the pig was about eight feet in front of them face to face with his hackles up. Before I could do anything the pig was at my legs.

I only had a .22 and all I could do was back up pushing myself off the track into the thick manuka and fire two shots point bank into the pig. He turned and raced down through a small swamp and up into the manuka again. I had assumed that he had charged at the dogs and hadn't seen me, attacking me by mistake. I raced down through the swamp, and scrambled up on a track on my hands and knees though the manuka, when suddenly I heard him coming towards me, huffing noisily as he rapidly approached. I barely had time to scramble to my feet, get off the track and squeeze into the tight manuka, when he was once again going for my legs. I again fired two shots point blank range into him and all he did was turn and head back where he had come from. I realised then that he had come back looking for me. By then the dogs were barking and I heard a battle going on. I climbed a tree for a better view and saw the pig and the dogs spinning in circles on a small green grassy knob. Richard was close by and fired a shot. But he missed. I shouted out, "Don't shoot while the dogs are in there!". However, he fired again and killed the pig. Luckily the dogs and I were unharmed.

We gutted the boar, but found it was too heavy to carry out. We hung it up in the manuka to stop the meat from going off. Richard said he would collect it the next day in his short wheel base Landrover, which was a very early model and unsuitable for travelling long distances because it was too slow and uncomfortable which is why we had left it behind initially. When Richard returned the next day he found he couldn't get to the pig because the clay tracks were far too greasy for the vehicle to negotiate. So he lost it.

After that Richard and I went on several trips together and on another trip, also at a Waiau, a different property this time, we took an old 4WD army truck that I owned but was very slow as well as uneconomical. My son Glen, with Richard driving, left an hour before me so they would get there around the same time as me. I took my car.

I was reminded that day why I didn't like carrying a rifle. We were on a small ridge, when one of Richard's dogs started fossicking in a flax bush about 50 yards ahead of us across a small gully. Thinking it was possums he was after, Richard started to yell at his dog. I just had time to say "Hang on a moment" when a black boar flew out and chased the dog. He then stood still while the dog bailed it. I had my .303 with me which was not my normal practice as they are a nuisance when running after dogs. They can become caught up in scrub and slow your progress. I upped with the rifle and fired a shot. Immediately I knew I shot over the top of him. We were too close. My half bulldog Sooty appeared right there and then grabbed the pig. It was another nice boar.

Later that same day the dogs went up a big bush gully. There were a few barks and they were chasing something. So I sat down and waited on the side of the hill where there were patches of manuka scrub. I hadn't waited long when I saw a flash between two patches of manuka. I quickly brought my rifle up and followed the progress of the boar. There were only two gaps in which I could get a shot, and after following them through the scope I kept the cross hairs on the tip of the pig's nose and squeezed the trigger. But the pig kept going. I had only one more opportunity when he passed through the last gap between two patches of scrub. The same thing happened again, I lined him up and pulled the trigger, but he kept going. I thought he was gone forever.

When my dog Sooty appeared two or three minutes later behind the pig, I tried to call him back. It was a waste of time continuing the chase because the pig was too far ahead, or so I thought. But when Sooty had only just disappeared from sight he let out a couple of barks, then stopped. Something was strange, so I went down there and found the pig dead with Sooty standing beside it. One shot had just grazed it across the back and the second one was through the kidneys. This gave me a bit more confidence with my shooting. However I still preferred to let others use the guns – I liked to look after our dogs and I preferred to use my bayonet. I was quite happy – especially if I was on my own hunting – if the dogs couldn't get the pig, it deserved to get away.

Another young man, Bob Brett, whom I met in similar circumstances, that is, he was keen, had somewhere to go hunting, but no one to go with, arranged with me to go with him to hunt a property near Arthur's Pass. It was an easy drive out the back on a 4WD track, where we got a nice black boar. It was the first wild pig Bob had ever seen. The dogs bailed it and held it, and Bob got to stick it. It was a hundred and fifty pounder. We took it home to Bob's place and he took a lot of photos. Not long after that I called over to see him one evening and I could see him through the gaps in the curtains of French doors asleep on the couch, but my knocking could not awaken him. I went around to the back door which was unlocked and let myself in. Bob's wife worked shifts and was not home. Bob seemed to be breathing heavily. I hadn't known him long, and didn't know if he may have been on some sort of medication so I decided not to disturb him and went home. During the night it played on my mind a little bit. I hoped he was ok. At 8.00 am next morning his wife rang and said that Bob had died. He had been taken to the hospital, overnight, but taken off life support. It was a shock. When I told her that I had seen him and thought he was asleep she assured me that there was nothing I could have done. Bob was only in his early thirties with a young family. It was tragedy for them. I was glad I had helped Bob to fulfil his wish to kill a wild pig.

JACK PAYNE

Jack Payne had a farm on the Kaikoura Inland Road. He was a very sociable chap and allowed us to go hunting on his property. So he was obviously one of the good guys.

Diesel Dan had arranged a trip for a weekend and as the time approached, we weren't sure how we were going to travel up there – his car or mine. We were going to have to tow the Gnat with the dogs in the dog-box and about a day before we were due to go Dan purchased a 1954 Austin A70 which was very cheap, he said, and we could use that. He bought it for seventeen pounds ten shillings and it went well.

After we finished work on the Friday we packed our gear and put the dogs in the trailer and we were off, stopping only for the pubs on the way. First stop Amberley, next, Waipara and so on. So I guess you could call it a pub-crawl.

Before you reach Jack's house there is a river to cross and we arrived at this river at about one a.m. Dan was asleep in the passenger seat. When I pulled up at the river and had a look at what was ahead I could see that it was in full flood. I shook Dan and woke him up and said, "What do you reckon about this?" Dan just sat up, took one look, and said, "She'll be right," and went straight back to sleep!

So putting it into the crawler first gear, I started through the water which was a lot deeper than I expected. It came halfway up the doors and I thought that any minute the car would stop or start missing, but it never missed a beat, probably due to it being a very tall motor, with the distributor out of the way. Anyway, for whatever reason, it did better than I thought. The house is about another one hundred and fifty metres further on, and we pulled up next to the sleep-out we were expecting to stay in for the next few nights, grabbed our sleeping bags, opened the door and saw that two of the three beds were occupied by the farmer's son and a friend. Daniel was pretty much under the weather so he went straight to sleep while I went back to the car and slept the night in it.

In the morning Dan came out to get me and we went over and knocked on the door of the house to be greeted by Jack's wife who was a really lovely lady. She told us that Jack had only just got home, he had arrived soaking wet and freezing cold, and it was then we learned his story.

Jack had been into Kaikoura to replenish his beer supplies but on the way home he had had an unfortunate accident. He had hit the railing of the crib Creek Bridge, putting it through the bonnet of his 1947 Chevrolet. The weather was very cold, not the sort in which you would want to be stuck out in overnight. In those days there was very little traffic on the shingle road, especially at that late hour but this must have been his lucky night because he managed to get assistance from a couple of young guys in their car who took him as far as the ford in the river, and left him there. Jack wasn't too far from home, about a hundred metres, and started off wading across the ford in the dark. Next minute he was being swept away downstream and into some willows where he floundered around trying to find his way in the moonless night.

He said he had nearly given up when he saw a car pull up, hesitate, and then drive through the water. He told us that he thought to himself, "I must be down at the neighbour's place because no-one can get across my ford." The previous week he had left his tractor on one side of the river, and his car on the other, and he realized when he headed towards the ford that he knew where he was. In the early hours of the morning he staggered in, very pleased for the warmth of his home.

Dan and I had gone there for the sole purpose of pig hunting, but Jack had a job for us first. We had to take him back to his car and retrieve his stash of flagons. He had them planted under bushes and all around the place. They were in such a variety of places we had to make sure we didn't miss any. When we arrived back at his house he asked us if we would like a beer and it was gratefully accepted. Jack poured us a small beer each, put the top back on the flagon, and went and put it away. I could see we weren't going to get anymore so we decided it was time to go pig hunting even though it was getting a bit late in the day and near lunchtime.

Jack's old pet deaf dog was a lovely friendly Dalmatian, too friendly in fact, because the dog kept an eye on us and loved coming with us when we went out for a hunt. This would have been ok except that he loved possums and it was useless yelling at him because he was as deaf as a post, and even sign language didn't deter him. So there we were, trying to get a pig, and the Dalmatian was trying to retrain our dogs for us as we started to head out to the back of the farm. He was a dear old dog but a darn nuisance

The next day we started out early and there was a frost with the sun streaming down, and blue skies and we had a decent early start. We only got one pig, Dan shot a couple of deer and although we continued on after he shot the deer in the hope of getting another pig, we didn't. The ground had been frozen when we started out in the morning, and it was now a lovely warm day, and before we got back to the car carrying our deer the ground had started to freeze

Daniel and me and Jack's dear old deaf Dalmation.

again and I remember lying on the frosty ground with sweat pouring off me with the exertion, but it was well worth it. We got seventeen pounds ten shillings at the game packers' depot, so all in all we were happy and felt we had had a very successful trip.

HARRY AND REWI

It is always interesting when you are a stranger to the area to pull up outside a small town pub with a trailer full of dogs and with pigs on board. It doesn't take long before the locals are deserting their beers to have a gander at what's parked outside, and to give their expert opinions as to how good your dogs would perform against the pigs in their area.

This was how we met Harry Powell and Rewi Pacey at the Amberley Hotel.

Harry was forty, of solid build and about six feet tall, and quite proud of the fact that his doctor had predicted his early demise if he did not cut back on his drinking, and that he would be lucky to live till forty. To him, reaching forty was a great milestone in his life and proved to Harry that doctors don't know everything.

Harry boasted that there were three-hundred pound pigs where he hunted, and they would soon kill all our dogs, so being young enthusiastic fellows, we were quick to take up the challenge, and Harry arranged a trip to Hunua.

Harry knew all about pigs, and was very set in his ways. For instance, he reckoned it was no use starting out too early. "You've been doing it all wrong," is what Harry said. "Pigs are like humans, they've all got hangovers in the mornings, and ten a.m. is an early enough start time!"

So it was ten a.m. when I arrived at Harry's home in my Morris 1000 with my young son, Glen who was about seven or eight at the time. After picking Harry up, he said, "I've just got to go around and pick up my mate first from the Railway Hotel." We pulled up outside the pub, and were met by a friend of Harry's who had a quick look at the car's three occupants and said, "I have got a four and a half gallon keg (of beer). Do you think that will be enough?"

I told him it would be enough as my son was only a small drinker anyway! After assuring them that their beer would be quite safe, and promising not to drink it all, we proceeded on our way. By this time of the day it had become very warm, as it was mid-summer and would have been a day better spent lazing on the beach, but I was still keen for my dogs Dinda and Saki to have a run, and to get a pig for the sake of my young son Glen.

We drove up a farm track until Harry told us where to stop. As we pulled up, I could see that these two guys with us couldn't wait to get stuck into the keg, and had no interest in walking anywhere. So while Harry and his friend sat drinking beer in the hot sun, Glen and I started walking through open farmland with rolling hills and matagouri gullies, until we managed to get one small piglet, and decided it was too hot to continue, so returned to the car.

While it was not a complete disaster it was not my idea of hunting. I like to be on site before daybreak when the dew is on the grass and the scents are fresh.

Another drinking companion of Harry's was Rewi Pacey, who owned the local fish and chip shop. Rewi had caught polio as a child, was about five foot six tall, wiry in build, wore a brace on one leg, and walked with a limp, but he was a gutsy little fellow so when Harry arranged pig hunting trips Rewi liked to be included.

Harry arranged a trip for us to go up Greenwoods on the Amberley sea coast and Dan and I took the Gnat. I was the driver, but Rewi insisted on walking because he thought the Gnat was unsafe, until we came to an uphill face covered in knee-high matagouri where I managed to talk Rewi into getting on board. We were going well for a while until, nearing the top of the hill, the Gnat reared up. Before

I could stop it, the Gnat had done a backward flip and pinned the pair of us down in the thorns. Neither of us were hurt, but there was no way I could get Rewi back in that Gnat.

Harry had a dog, a black and white collie with one wall eye, and while standing talking as we surveyed the countryside I accidentally stood on one of his dog's toes. It reacted like lightening, grabbing me on the anklebone, striking a nerve and temporarily paralysing my foot completely. I hopped around on one leg swearing and calling the dog all the bad names in the book and I got absolutely no sympathy from its owner. "Well, you stood on his foot – what do you expect?" I know that none of our dogs would have reacted like that.

As far as getting the big dog-killing boars that Harry promised, the only big boar that we got was on Daniel's first trip to Hunua with Harry, Rewi and their friends. I was not there on that occasion, but assumed that they would have taken plenty of liquid refreshments.

Flock Hill. Bob Brett's Boar 150lbs.

CHAPTER 13

Good Dogs I Have Known

ANY DOG THAT CAN GET you a pig on its own has earned the title of "pig dog" and, as with owners, they come in various shapes and sizes and abilities. Over the years I have seen some exceptional dogs for various reasons and there are a number of qualities that I look for when choosing a dog.

1. Must be controllable and trustworthy with stock
2. Work well with other dogs (no trouble makers)
3. Not get injured and be forever at the vets
4. Should be hunting for you and the pack
5. Should not go for miles without you
6. Must use its eyes ears and nose
7. Must have a good brain and be intelligent
8. Must have stamina and good hard feet
9. Should be a colour easily visible in open country

Consider sharing dogs with a friend because it is the experience and work that makes them. As in a football team one dog can complement another. A wind-finder will pick up the scent on the air and go straight to the source, while a ground-scenting dog will follow the path the animal has taken. Both may get there, but depending on the country the wind-finder is usually first to the animal.

If you don't want to carry a rifle, just a knife or bayonet, it is hard to go past a bully- cross. My favourites are British bulldog-crosses or working dog Labrador-crosses or even some Labrador-spaniel-crosses or Foxy-crosses and Greyhound-crosses. (Greyhounds are known as gaze hounds in America because of their good eyesight.)

Ray Thomson, a hunting mate from Kaikoura, had an exceptional dog called Roy. Roy was given to Ray as a pup by some people who had come down from the North Island to muster wild cattle from the back of Conway Hills, at five pounds per head, and Roy was descended from their pack of dogs. Roy would normally walk with you until he picked up a scent. When he went, ninety-nine times out of a hundred, he found something and was very good at catching deer. Jack Barker told me that Roy was the only dog he had ever seen catch a stag running uphill. To look at he was just a tri-coloured farm dog type, much like you would see anywhere around the country, but he could catch pigs and deer. I saw him one day chasing after a deer that ran down a creek below me. Although the deer had a good head start, he soon had it bailed in a pool close to where the creek ran into a main river.

When Roy bailed, he howled, but not like an ordinary dog. His howl was very distinctive and could be heard for miles.

On a pig-hunting trip at Kaikoura, Ray with his two dogs Roy, and Tip, which was a black and white border collie-cross, were walking along a ridge covered in thick bush on either side, when Roy got on to a large red stag which was in the velvet, and running back and forth through the trees with his head held back so as not to damage his soft antlers. Ray really wanted to get a pig, so continued on without Roy, thinking the dog might tire of his game and catch up, but he never did. It was several hours later while returning down the same ridge that Ray could hear Roy howling in the one spot. Upon investigation he found his dog had the stag down. The poor deer had been run to a standstill, so all that was required was to cut the stag's throat and carry it out which was no easy task as it weighed over two hundred and twenty pounds. Ray said he sold it and got more for the velvet than he did for the carcass.

Mate was another exceptionally good dog owned by Des Campbell and used by myself whenever possible. He was a black rough-coated staghound pointer-cross, an excellent finder and bailer, a good holder when needed, trustworthy and brainy. On a hunting trip with my good friends, brothers John and David Whiting, we were gazing

Des's Dog 'Mate', a Staghound Cross. One of the very best!

out over some hilly tussock county from a high vantage point at Waiau when my eye caught a slight movement in the tussocks several hundred metres below us. After watching for a while, we ascertained there was a mob of pigs sunbathing below us. Desperate to keep the dogs in and not give the pigs any warning, the three of us scuttled from one patch of cover to another while the dogs became more and more excited until in the end we could hold them back no longer, and there were pigs and dogs running in all directions. David shot a big sow, and Mate looked magnificent bounding alongside a large grey boar as they ran around the hillside and into some thick manuka where the boar got into a steep-sided muddy wallow.

With three dogs bailing inches from his nose, the boar's attention was fully taken. However, I hesitated about jumping into the wallow with him when I saw the thickness of his hocks, which would have been difficult to get your hands around, and they had mud on them. I wondered for a moment if I would be able to hold him if he played up. No hesitation from Mate though; he stopped barking, walked backwards a few paces and walked in a large semi-circle until he was with me, behind the pig. Then immediately he grabbed the pig by the ear at the same time as I stuck it. It was another good boar around the one hundred and eighty pound mark, and this convinced me that some dogs have brains enough to solve problems on their own without instruction. It was as if the dogs had extra-sensory perception and knew your thoughts.

Anyway, there are plenty of good dogs out there just waiting to be discovered, but you still need to give them the work.

My old bulldog bitch Jean had a litter to Cass, Maurie Smith's bull terrier greyhound-cross. At the time I thought if nothing else they will at least be holders, but they all started finding early. Pip, the pup I kept from the litter, found and held his first pig at five months of age after I had taken him to a friend's pig sty and put him in with a pen of porkers which were just a little bit bigger than the

TOP: Maurie Smith with Cass, Pip and Darkie. BOTTOM: Adam (Dave Whiting's stepson) and I and a couple of good pigs, 170 lbs and 250 lbs.

pup. He ignored them for a while, sniffing around the four corners of the pen until the pigs became interested in him and he gave one a nip and it squealed. It was as if a light-switch had been thrown. I grabbed Pip and threw him out of the pen, but he immediately jumped back in, so I carried him out and put him back in the trailer. After that, if we were in pig country he was looking for them which was challenging with just a bayonet and no firearm.

I did have one other dog at the time. Eight months-old Ricky, my liver and white staghound springer spaniel-cross, was also hunting well and I was hunting with others who had dogs, but we usually separated to cover more country. Pip's first wild pig was a big sow, which I let go as I found I had lost my bayonet on the way down the hill. Despite searching, I never saw it again, so had no way of killing it. Pip, at this stage thought it was some sort of a game, but it wasn't long before things became serious. He got the message and thoroughly enjoyed pig hunting after that.

There are plenty of good dogs looking for work but they should be socialized from an early age and taught to hunt only what you want. A dog will do a lot more for an owner who looks after him, and respects him. I was given a boxer Labrador-cross which the owner, a security guard, thought might make a good pig dog. He was getting rid of him because he was getting a pair of German Shepherds, but the dog threatened to attack any person who approached me too quickly and he also could not be trusted with stock so he was given back.

Another dog I owned which had no vices, other than going too far away, was a huntaway pointer-cross which I gave to a couple of fit young hunters just starting their hunting career.

Nero, a dog of indeterminate breed, was another good dog that I owned. He had a chubby body which resembled a bull terrier's, and was black with a smooth coat but he had a fine terrier-type face with whiskers. He was an excellent finder and the minute you laid your hands on the pig he'd bailed, he was on to the next one.

So you had to be young and fit to keep up with him.

Pig dogs come in all shapes and sizes and are whatever works for you. As a young man I didn't want any half-hearted dogs tagging along for the ride nor did anyone in their right mind want to own a dog that cost a fortune in vet bills every time you ran across a boar. In other words whether or not the dog had brawn it must have brains and know its own limitations. It also needs to have an exceptional sense of smell whether it tracks through scenting the air or following a ground scent or a combination of both. Of course you could own a dog that potentially could be the best dog in the world, but it won't be unless you give it the work. This means you need somewhere with plentiful game to get started, then a variety of country to hunt from, Murchison-type, with a combination of big fern-covered faces to mature bush and broken rocky areas to forestry blocks, to larger open tussock country. Some dogs obviously prefer one type to another the same way that their owners do. Two or three dogs working well together can be as good as any number. Some dogs are tireless workers and can go for days while others can slow down considerably after a hard day on the hills.

Ricky, my liver and white springer spaniel-cross, had great stamina. You could see that when the rest of the pack were fresh Ricky would get upset if any other dogs ran ahead while he had his nose to the ground. He loped along always with his nose down. If you went away to hunt for several days the more tired the other dogs became, the better Ricky would perform.

As a keen pig hunter for most of my life you can imagine the joy I felt when I applied for and landed a job as a dog ranger for the Christchurch City Council. My full-time job for twenty-five years prior to this had been as a roofer, but I felt I could do with a change as roofing and pig hunting are equally demanding physically and I enjoy talking with people and working with all animals, dogs in particular. Having access to so many dogs can be frustrating as it is impossible to save every unwanted dog in such a large city, but we did try. At different times different types of breeds can be the most popular or most common. They come in waves of popularity from German-Shepherds to Dobermans to Rottweiler, to Pit-bulls, to Mastiffs or any other breed you can imagine.

There were no rip collars, tracking devices, quad bikes or farm bikes in those days, and four-wheel drive vehicles were rare unless you owned a farm because they were so expensive. Dan Robin and I both had Morris Minors for hunting wagons for quite some time, and then I had a Singer Gazelle, and a 1947 V8. Also a lot of farms didn't have the tracks they have today. I envy the modern, technology-equipped hunter as there were a couple of times I lost my dogs although I could hear them barking. Every time I ran in the direction of the sound I would lose it, go back up the hill and could hear them again, run twice as far next time without success, never to find where they went. The same thing happened on two different properties, both times I was on the top of a hill, the bailing loud and clear, but the further you ran the less noise until it stopped completely, go back, the dogs still barking furiously: very frustrating.

Just about any bulldog-cross will work, but the younger the better when you start putting time into their training. A foxy or spaniel-cross will cover a lot of country, be cheap on the dog tucker, and they tend to live a long time, relatively trouble-free. In my experience I have found that the heavier breeds, as they age, can have problems with collapsing from exhaustion in hot weather. A friend's bull mastiff staghound-cross used to do it, as did Carl, my Great Dane-Labrador cross. Believe me, it is no fun having to carry a large dog out, and then there is the problem of finding them if they go down out of sight.

Some of the best pig dogs have been freebies or twenty dollar pups. Be wary of sellers offering dogs for sale unless someone with experience can vouch for both the seller and the dogs. A few years back someone placed an ad in the Christchurch *Press* saying they had a pack of pig dogs for sale, and would only be in town for the weekend as they were passing through on their way down south to a new job in Mataura, so couldn't give a trial. A young guy I had been out with a couple of times and had no dogs, saw the ad and believing everything the owner told him, paid cash and bought a brown and white mongrel bitch about twelve months old. We took it hunting a few days later and it was obvious from the start it had never been off the tar-seal. It wouldn't cross creeks, and was reluctant to go up and down steep bits. Needless to say when the buyer returned to the address where he had picked up the dog there was no one there. House vacant!

If you're just starting out, get advice from someone with experience and good dogs. Most would be only too pleased to help, and chuffed that you had asked them. I have seen dogs that would attack their owner if he went near the dead pig, dogs that would chase pigs away, and would only bark if the pig was at least a hundred metres ahead, and this is hard to find out if you are hunting in dense bush. I once went out with a friend whose dog would attack my finder while he was bailing but I didn't find the problem out until I saw it happening in the open country. Before that I had been in the forest where Ricky had a pig that got away after the other dog went down to it, and I heard what sounded like a bit of a skirmish between the dogs.

Once I was attacked by one of our own dogs which caused the rest of the pack to support him as I tried to carry a live fawn back to the car. I tried hitting out at the main culprit with a Manuka stick but it only made things worse and they weren't happy until they had dragged the fawn from my shoulders and killed it. The instigator was Prince, a pure bred black Labrador. I stopped taking him out after that.

While working as a dog ranger there came a time when the Pound keeper was going on annual leave, and I volunteered to do his duties for part of the holiday. Now John, the Pound keeper was of swarthy complexion and Spanish origin, and all he ever spoke about when going there to book in a stray dog was the Spanish civil war and the evils of Franco – John was obviously an expert on this subject. If he wasn't, he sure had us fooled. His other passion was breeding chow-chows, which I had always found unfriendly and distrustful of strangers, but he was a good Pound keeper and had earned a break. For my part, I was quite happy to do another's job for a change.

At that time the City Council pound was in the same grounds as the SPCA in Wilmers Road, but had separate offices and pens. The pens were about eight by ten metres, and each would house six to eight animals without much trouble. The sides were cyclone netting about seven feet tall, which at the top cantilevered out at an upward angle to deflect and discourage any would-be jumpers. At one end was a lane from which the public could view the dogs and at the other end of the pens, a shelter from any bad weather. My first job in the morning was to pick up the poos, hose out, then disinfect the runs and finally feed the dogs a few biscuits each.

I had two pups around twelve-months old who were both going well on the pigs, and it became my daily habit to throw them in the back of the truck and take them to work, letting them out for a short run whenever I had the time. By about noon all the chores were finished and there was time for lunch before opening to the public at one p.m.

I had a quick bite to eat then let the pups out for run around the grounds, when a member of the public arrived and we started chatting. After about five minutes I suddenly realised my dogs had disappeared, and were nowhere to be seen or heard. Next minute it dawned on me, "Oh my gawd, there's a free range pig farm right next door, that's where they'll be," and sure enough as we ran toward the boundary fence I heard a muffled bark. The farm was in a depression, in an old shingle pit down a steep bank, and we hadn't heard any noises earlier. When I looked, I could hardly believe my eyes, here's Pip on the ear and Rick bailing hard on the nose, but was it a weaner? No way, the paddock was filled with giant breeding sows, and they had singled out the boar, which was a monster and none too happy about these intruders in his backyard. Luckily, I got a helping hand from the customer I had been talking to, so I was able to pass Rick to him to hang on to while I got Pip off. He kicked and squealed like a schoolgirl as I carried him away, but no way was I going to put him down. He received a couple of minor flesh wounds, nothing to go to the vet about. He was lucky. I told the farmer what had happened, but he was very good about it, and there were no repercussions, thank God.

While minding the Pound there was one dog that kept escaping, he was a real Houdini. Every morning it would be at the office

Pig Hunter Karl – a Great Dane cross.

door awaiting my arrival. If I spoke softly to it and told it to get behind the counter it would. If I told it to lie down at the front it would. No hand signals, no raised voices, no having to repeat the command. This dog was magic. If I had needed any convincing, all doubts were dispelled the day I found him a new owner. You see, every night as I locked up and left the Pound, I endeavoured to make sure he didn't escape. I chained him in – he still met me next morning at the office door, so as a last resort I chained him up in our killing room, which was at the end of one of the dog runs and shut the door.

Next morning, surprise, surprise, the dog was waiting for me again. Now, I had never witnessed him getting out of the run, let alone any of the other obstacles I had placed in his path, and if I put him back in the run and told him to stay there, he would, until I had left for the day. Eventually his time was up, and he remained unclaimed so he could go to a new home. I thought about keeping him, but I already had enough dogs.

One day a man came in with a young family asking if we had any setters or retrievers as he lived in the country near Lake Ellesmere, We didn't, so I told him about our collie-cross, but he said he wasn't interested, so I said he should have a look anyway. The collie was in with a half dozen others. The dog and I looked one another in the eye, and softly I said three words, "Come on out," then right before my eyes for the very first time I watched as he climbed up the netting and swung himself up and over the projection at the top which was meant to stop this happening. He then walked along the centre rail until he could jump down on the outside. Needless to say, everyone was impressed, and since then I have often thought of that dog and wondered what became of him, and wished I had given him a trial. As Joe, a friend of mine used to constantly remind me, "You should have kept him."

TOP LEFT: Cass with Maurie, and Jean the bulldog bitch.
BOTTOM: Wok, the bulldog cross.

TOP: Pip, the bulldog greyhound cross, an excellent finder and holder.
BOTTOM: Me with the dogs at Glen Colwyn.

CHAPTER 14

Early Memories

AS THIS BOOK WAS WRITTEN as a legacy for my children as well as entertainment for family and friends, I am closing with one final chapter – mainly about my early childhood and teenage years.

My father's parents were farmers in Kaikoura, but his granny, his paternal grandmother, brought up my father in Christchurch because his mother died three weeks after his birth, leaving her husband with seven children to rear.

I was born in Christchurch in 1938, to Guy and Nance Broadhurst, and with my sister Lorna we lived in 140 Olivier's Road, Linwood. We never saw very much of my father's family in Kaikoura because we didn't have a car in those days. Cars were not so common, the roads were twisty and winding with one-way bridges and unsealed, and my father's method of transport was a pushbike which he rode to his place of employment, a twenty-six mile round trip to Templeton and back.

I can still remember the soldiers parading past our home during the Second World War, and from the early 1940's having to block the windows at nights, with towels and sheets to make sure no light shone through, as it was feared the enemy was not far from New Zealand's shores. It was called "the blackout" and every home had to do it. We lived in a one-bedroom flat, with my younger sister and me and my parents having to share the same bedroom. My father spent the war in Tonga in Nuku'alofa in the Artillery, but they never saw any action to the best of my knowledge. My sister Lorna always remembers that on the day he finally came home: a man pushed open the window of the bedroom and threw his kit bag inside, and she asked him who he was. He said, "I'm your father," and she said, "No, you're not, my father's at the war!"

I was only five years old and in primer one at school when I fell in love for the first time. The little girl's name was Carol and was from a large family of girls. We walked home together most days, and at the corner of Olivier's Road and Cashel Street we had to separate because we lived in different streets. One day I said to her, "I will give you my penny if you give me a kiss." We sneaked behind the portal of the nearby church on the corner. I gave her a quick peck on the cheek, handed her the penny, and we both ran off in different directions. I wonder if she ever told her mother.

The brick church where I had kissed my sweetheart no longer exists as it was demolished as a result of the Christchurch earthquakes in 2011.

Years later I met up with Carol's sister, Beverley, at a school class reunion. I told her what we did and Beverley laughed and said, "What a little tart!" She told me that Carol had married a man called Warwick!

My father's cousin Isobel had married Dick Moore whose father Bill had a dairy farm in Macgregor's Road, and supplied the surrounding neighbourhood with milk and cream. I would go and sit on an old black horse, Billy. He was in his thirties and on his last legs, and I would sit on him for hours at a time, pat him and talk to him, and he was a dear old thing. But Prince, the draft horse, wasn't so lovable. He would try and bite me while I sat on Billy's back and chase me if I was on foot in the paddock. Prince was the draft horse they used to pull the dray they used for haymaking, and he had a mean disposition.

Luckily, there were lupins in his paddock to hide behind for a bit of cover if you passed through. Another horse kept in a separate paddock was Kitty, and she pulled the milk cart. The milk and cream was dispensed with pint and quart dippers from the cans on the milk cart into the billy-cans which were left at the gate. I just loved to go with Dick on the milk round in the early hours of the morning, so much so that I would sneak out of the window, barefoot, short pants and just a flannelette short-sleeved shirt, get on my bike to arrive in time for the milk run.

Another memory of Kitty was of Dick placing me in front of him on the horse without the saddle and bridle, and he held me while we galloped around the paddock, pulling up abruptly at a fence, Kitty putting her head down, and me sliding over the front, and down partially over her neck, until Dick grabbed me and pulled me back up. The horse was a hard worker, being used not just for the milk run, but also for taking the bobby calves to Belfast Freezing Works, which was about a ten-mile round trip pulling the gig, a large-wheeled buggy with hard rubber tyres. For those who are unfamiliar with the term gig, it had a single seat, with a foot-well in front of you, and a small tray with sides at the back to carry the bobby calves.

Every Wednesday a mob of cattle driven by men on horseback would come down Harrow Street into Tuam Street heading for the sale yards. They probably numbered about forty to fifty and made quite a mess on the road. But no one ever complained. The residents would come out with their buckets and shovels and pick up the manure to fertilise their gardens.

Bordesley Street crossed Harrow Street, and dad's granny, who brought him up, lived in a house on the north east corner opposite Wislang's store, while his Aunt Nance and Uncle Tom lived at 104 Bordesley Street. Uncle Tom and Aunt Nance were very good to me because they allowed me to keep a number of pets in their back yard, and Uncle Tom helped me to build a pigeon loft. I also kept Chinese silky bantams and Muscovy ducks which were hatched out by the bantams. I always remember Uncle Tom telling me when he was a boy there was nothing but lupins and sandhills from there all the way to the sea. Hence the soil was very poor, and the horse poo helped enrich the land. At that time the council used the land for paddocks to keep their draft horses, and the local kids built their huts there. Uncle Tom had a good garden because he collected the horse manure from the paddocks. He put it in a forty-four gallon drum, and kept topping it up with water and made a slurry out of it which he would pour on his garden with his watering can. Nowadays the whole area is the site of Linwood High School.

Every week Smith's City Market had a poultry auction. To a young boy this was very exciting. At one point I decided I would bid, thinking I would buy one bird. I won the bid before I realised I had bought a whole cage full! I had only wanted the one to add to my little flock that I had acquired from a Pigeon-racing enthusiast who lived down the road. Thankfully someone at the auction took pity on me and relieved me of the rest!

I had the pigeons for a year or so when I decided then to take them on their first major journey, so took them on the train to Timaru a hundred miles away and released them, anticipating their return shortly afterwards, maybe even beating me home. However, to my utter dismay and disappointment not one of them ever showed up!

For my seventh birthday in 1945, I received a half-sized two-wheeler bike. It was a big outlay for my parents, as they weren't wealthy. I was attending Linwood Primary School at the time, and one day a friend and I were on our bikes outside the school gates when we saw clouds of smoke from a large fire. From where we were it appeared to be just down Cashel Street, which was not too far away, and we headed off to investigate. It turned out to be the big fire at the Ballantyne's department store in which forty one workers died due to a lack of fire escapes. From where we stood on the north-east corner of Colombo and Cashel Streets we were very close to the action as we watched the firemen struggling to contain it. This event in November 1947 went down in history as one of New Zealand's worst disasters. Forty-one people died, and one of our immediate neighbours in Olivier's Rd was one of those who died in the fire.

Sometimes, on my way to school, I would walk by a house in Wellington Street where there was a little girl with dark curly hair and I would say hello to her. She turned out to be Yvonne Parker of the Parker and Hulme infamy. This little girl and her friend Juliet Hulme murdered Parker's mother in Victoria Park in June 1954. This remains one of Christchurch's most notorious crimes.

HOLIDAYS AT DUNTROON

Mum's elder sister Ngaio was married to Bill Brooker, whose occupation was a rabbiter at Duntroon, North Otago, and the highlight of the school holidays for me was to visit my aunty and uncle and cousins. We would travel by steam train to Oamaru, and Bill would pick my sister, mother and me up from the railway station, and take us to their home, a very small cottage surrounded by macrocarpa trees on McKenzie's property. The steam trains belched clouds of soot and smoke, and whenever there was a slight bend in the track we kids would stick our heads out the window to watch the engine at the front of the train, and inevitably get an eyeful of grit from the soot.

It was in the days of food rationing after the Second World War, and everyone had to have coupons to buy foods like butter and meat etc. On one trip down in the train, Mum had been saving butter coupons and filled her large leather shopping bag with her allowable quota to take to my aunt. Unfortunately the weather was hot, and the butter liquefied, making it inedible, so that was the end of that. Despite diligent scraping and washing, the leather bag never did completely lose the smell of the rancid butter.

My earliest recollection of going down there was with Uncle Bill in his 1927 Chevrolet Tourer. He had his dogs with him, and they had to lie on the running boards, which were covered in sacks. There were five children, three adults (as my father never came with us) and four dogs, all piled in and on and over the vehicle. I am sure that we forded a river at some stage, but I can't remember exactly where it was, but the road was shingle as most were in those days, and Uncle Bill pointed out a whole hillside covered in rabbits out for an evening nibble. The entire hillside appeared to be moving.

Because the cottage was so small we children used to make huts under the macrocarpa trees and sleep out at night, which was fine as long as it didn't rain. We would light a fire and make a damper with flour and water and cook it in the ashes, and nibble away on it between meals as we young kids were very hungry most of the time with using up so much energy and having fun doing it. One of my cousins was a girl, Jennifer. She was older than me, while the rest were younger. We were all roughly around similar ages, but the two boys, Gary and Alan, did not have the same interests in hunting as I did, so I would go out on my own every day I was allowed.

There was always something to do in the country, and for a young city boy it was very exciting. Uncle Bill was really kind to me, and used to take me around his trap lines with him. I couldn't wait to see what was caught in the traps. There was such a variety of creatures, ferrets, stoats, hawks, wild cats, and of course the real target, rabbits. Most of all I enjoyed being allowed to take the dogs on my own and go hunting for rabbits. If I had a good breakfast they wouldn't see me for lunch and I wouldn't return until late, in time for dinner. I would take the dogs down to the river bed which wasn't far from the house and chase rabbits all around the place, digging them out of nests and discovering other things like Pukeko's nests, and nests of wild kittens.

There were four dogs, two fox terriers, a female Irish water spaniel named Dawn, and an offspring of hers by a sheepdog, called Chips. One morning as I left to go down to the river with the dogs there were two or three sheep standing on the side of the road, and Chips chased them, so I turned back and told Uncle Bill that Chips had chased the sheep, and all he said was, "That's ok, leave him behind and you go hunting." I hadn't gone far down the road when I heard a rifle shot. I didn't ask, but I never saw Chips again.

On the way home after being out all day one of the fox terrier dogs disappeared into a large warren. I waited for thirty minutes, but he didn't come back out, and I was so worried I thought he was stuck, so I went back to tell my uncle and he said, "Don't worry, he will be alright," and he was quite right, the dog arrived back eventually none the worst for his adventure.

To make a bit of extra pocket money, we children would look for dead sheep and pluck the wool, and gather any caught on the barbed wire of the fences and then we would gather the wild mushrooms and take them into Oamaru by car and sell them. On one trip as we drove down into the town of Oamaru, the car did a sudden lurch and one of the back wheels came off and overtook the car. All I can remember is that we sat there for quite some time before Uncle Bill replaced the wheel and finally got us on our way again.

Another favourite pastime was gorging ourselves on the wild gooseberries which covered the riverbed at Livingston Pinch, a steep hill near the banks of the river. There were red gooseberries and yellow gooseberries, hairy gooseberries and smooth gooseberries, and my aunty used to make gooseberry jam with them. By the time I had been there for a fortnight my feet had hardened up sufficiently that I could walk through paddocks of thistles bare-footed.

When the weather was warmer and it rained, the river level would rise and we would all go down with car tubes and float and play in the water. Normally the river did not carry much water and we had to be content with looking for cock-a-bullies and eels for our entertainment, or exploring the nearby limestone formations which were full of fossilized shells, sea horses, and various other sea creatures.

Those early childhood holidays at Duntroon were fond memories and gave me an appreciation of the beauty of the countryside, and the pleasure of physical exercise and of exciting outdoor pursuits, a prelude to my pig hunting days as a young adult.

The boys I mixed with at school had a bad influence on me and I inevitably got into trouble. I set fire to a hedge in Linwood Park, and in the company of two other boys stole soft drinks from the Linwood school hall, which was used for dances and there were crates of drinks stashed there. A big temptation for a young fellow!

My nine year old friend and his eleven year old brother were from a large family of about seven boys. One of their older brothers had a Model T Ford, which he left parked in the driveway. We were caught one day by the boy's mother trying to push start it as we had the brilliant idea of driving it to Brighton, or anywhere! Imagine what it would look like to any observer to see three skinny little boys careering down the road, and the potential disaster that could have occurred if the mother hadn't stopped us.

Another day we lit a bonfire in their back yard and threw .22 calibre bullets into it, while we watched through the window of the house. Another favourite trick was that we put .22 calibre bullets on the tramline which ran past the end of their street.

We also tried running away from home, three of us on one pushbike with no warm clothing and no food. One sat on the handlebars, one on the bar and one doing the riding. Arthur thought we would take turns with the riding, but I couldn't get started because I was too small. So after heading out on the Akaroa Highway for a while, we turned right because we had no idea where we were going, and ended up at the Selwyn Bridge late in the day. We had planned in our childish minds to sleep in haystacks, steal a horse for riding, and raid orchards for food, but the wheels had fallen off our plans by then. Our plans had gone awry and there was no plan B.

By about five p.m. it was getting dark and we were all freezing cold and crying. All we wanted to do was go home again. We hadn't eaten a thing all day, so Arthur turned down the South Rd and we got as far back as Templeton, before he couldn't go any further so we turned ourselves in, and confessed our sins to the local garage proprietor, and luckily for us he was a good man and took us home to our parents in his car. The relatives had been very concerned and the police were there, ready to organize a search party.

After this, and with consultation within the family, my parents decided to separate me from my partners in crime, and I was sent to live with my cousin Dick Moore, whom I have already mentioned, and his wife Isobel who lived at Major Hornbrook Road, Mt Pleasant. They had no children of their own at that time, and they treated me like a son. This was like a whole new life for me, and it was a change for the better. The hills strengthened my legs walking to school and home every day.

Dick Moore was a hard-working and industrious man. Tall and wiry with angular features, he worked on the wharf at Lyttelton, He built his own home and grew flowers for sale on the adjoining section at Mount Pleasant. I was fortunate when I went to live with them for three years and attended Mount Pleasant school for standards four, five and six. It changed my life for the better.

Mount Pleasant School was small, with only about seventy pupils in total, mostly in the primers, and by the time I left there were only four boys and two girls in standard six, my final year.

The hills strengthened my legs, and I was fit and healthy. Dick was very good to me and taught me how to use woodworking tools, and gave me timber to play with and had me building sledges, which I used for sliding down the pine needle-coated ground in nearby Billie's Forest, now called Billie's Track.

I remember Dick telling me when I was a small child that it is a great thing to plant trees and this is something we should be doing. His words made some impact on me because when I had enough money in my mature years, I bought a block of land and planted a small forest. This has been an enjoyable interest for me over the years, as I have spent many a happy time planting and pruning.

HERBERT LE PAGE

Another good influence on my early life was Herbert Le Page. Herbert was an ex-Canterbury hockey representative and became our coach. He had arrived at Mount Pleasant School and asked if anyone would like to play hockey and he would be our coach. So it was hockey practice every break we got at school. We became very keen and would wolf our lunch down every day to make sure we had time for a quick game of hockey amongst ourselves before schoolwork resumed. Herbert was also the local carrier, and owned a truck with a canopy on the back, and carted all the boys to our hockey games with other schools every Saturday. The boys would pile in the back, some standing and some sitting. You would never get away with that nowadays.

The first year we came fairly high in the school's competitions, but the following year we won both the five-a-side schools championship, as well as the eleven-a-side championships. This was a tribute to the time and effort Mr. Le Page had put in for the boys. It was all voluntary work on his part, without him ever asking to be compensated.

I turned thirteen during my first year at Christchurch West High, but I never did enjoy school, neither the work nor the discipline. I couldn't wait to turn fifteen so I could leave. We had one teacher, Mr Feron, whose classroom was a prefab building next to the basketball courts in the playground. His idea of discipline bordered on outright cruelty. If a pupil was not looking at him in the classroom, his three-foot ruler would quickly come down on their knuckles, or a piece of chalk would bounce off their head. I remember one incident in particular. Ian, who had also come from Mount Pleasant and was unfortunately an asthmatic, was absolutely humiliated when he was caught glancing out the window at the girls doing gymnastics nearby. Feron roared at him, and made him go and put on girl's rompers and join the girls in their gymnastics. The poor boy turned scarlet, and unfortunately fellow pupils being only thirteen and insensitive at the time just laughed at him. Poor Ian, I felt the punishment was very inappropriate and certainly did not fit the crime.

My parents were against me leaving school but agreed to it provided I got a job, so a friend's father who worked for Norm Caldwell Builders and Joiners got me an apprenticeship starting in their joinery shop. I found it unbearable due to the sawdust and it resulted in me becoming asthmatic and I had to leave within a few months of starting. I had also by this time become interested in motorbikes, and one of the friends I had been in trouble with in an earlier life had one for sale. Unfortunately it couldn't have been any bigger. It was 1140cc, a Royal Enfield, and I sneaked fifteen pounds from my bank account and went around to buy it without ever having ridden a motorbike in my life

After the owner said, "No trouble, I'll teach you how to ride it," my lessons consisted of a quick trip the length of Ensor's Road, and back, with me peering over his shoulder trying to find out how different things worked, and hanging on for grim death as we rocketed down Ensor's Road and back to Havelock St where they lived. "There you go," he said, "all yours."

So I rode it home in second gear, and at the first T intersection I came to I turned the throttle on rather than off, but learned quickly and no damage was done. It was too hard for a fifteen-year old to kick over, and I had trouble starting the bike. Just down the road from our house there was a drain, which passed under the road, and caused a rise in the footpath, and it allowed me, with the help of all the local kids, to push-start it. Once going I couldn't stop it, and finally the inevitable happened, and I was stopped in Johns Road by the traffic cops, no license, no warrant, and once again I was in trouble. My parents made me sell the bike as they said it was far too big for me, but would allow me to have a two-stroke, so I bought a CZ 150cc, the first of many more bikes I bought from Whiting and Waltho's. By this time I was working at H.C. Urlwins who manufactured electrical goods, and did metal spinning, turning discs of copper into electric jugs.

But once again, this CZ motorbike was a disaster, everywhere I went it broke down. I tried riding it to my Auntie's place at Duntroon in North Otago, and the first breakdown occurred at Dunsandel only a few miles out of Christchurch. I went to the local garage there and they got it going again for me only to have it break down again by Temuka, and then at St Andrews, slightly south of Timaru. It kept spitting back through the carburetor. I could not get it to go any faster than twenty miles per hour. Each service station I took it to mucked around with it, and got it going again, but the problem recurred. I stayed the night at the hotel at St Andrews, and next morning back-tracked to Timaru to have it fixed again at a motorcycle shop, and once again I headed for Oamaru. I arrived at Oamaru leaving a trail of debt in my wake, and promptly bought a rail ticket for myself and the bike to be freighted back to Christchurch. I had had enough of that bike by then and put my name on a waiting list for an ex-Traffic Department 650 BSA Gold Flash as the council was replacing all the motorcycles. I would go in every Thursday on payday to Bond and Hockley BSA agents who sold the bikes on behalf of the council, and give them five pounds of my hard earned money towards my deposit on the new second hand bike, until at last it was passed over to me and I was the proud owner.

On my first night with my new bike I had a few close shaves and learned that you don't cross tramlines on an angle because the rails are very slippery and I got into a bit of a slide but managed to correct it in time. One evening during my first week of ownership, I rode down to the clock tower at New Brighton, which was a gathering place for the milk-bar cowboys. I knew one or two of them already, and because my bike was an ex-traffic cop's bike I was challenged to a race which I accepted even though I didn't have a clue where the race they had in mind was to go. I was unfamiliar with the streets at that time. It turned out to be north up Marine Parade, left at the old Ozone Hotel, and left again at Shaw Avenue, and then left again to complete the circuit down Seaview Road back to the clock tower. It was a real shambles, as I didn't know where the corners were, so needless to say I couldn't win.

A friend of mine, Wally Gibson, bought a proper factory racing Triumph, and was quite keen to have me ride it. After some fast riding down Ferry Road I decided to go over to Governors Bay, a road I regularly used as a racetrack! I was on my own this day, and in one of my moments of madness I decided I would see how quickly I could ride from Governors Bay to Lyttelton. So after having a quick glance at the time on my wristwatch, I took off like a maniac, cutting all the corners, scraping the foot pegs at every opportunity, racing up hill and down dale and taking extreme risks.

As I roared down the hill into Rapaki, I noticed a man working in a field. He took a double take and stood staring in amazement as he watched me flash by on my roaring flying machine. Around all the bends between Corsair Bay and Lyttelton, and into the Main Street of Lyttelton, I jammed on the brakes, stopped quickly and pulled off my gauntlet glove to reveal my time. To my absolute horror and disgust it showed exactly the same time as when I had left Governors Bay. My watch had stopped!

It was such a dangerous idiotic thing to do. I never attempted to do it again.

COLIN HURRELL AND RICKY MAINE

Colin Hurrell, someone I knew from our common interest in motorcycles, had a 500cc Matchless, which he had stripped of anything he deemed unnecessary, no lights, no mudguards, and no silencer. Colin and his bike were the scourge of the neighborhood: seeing how far he could spin the wheel, irritating anyone who wasn't stone deaf by seeing how much noise he could make, and regularly being chased home by the traffic department. They lived in an old square house, which was within three feet of their right-hand side boundary fence. If you looked up the side of the house the only thing stopping a view of the backyard was the position of the old outside lavatory. If you just rode your bike up there normally there was plenty of room between it and the side of the house, but one of Colin's practices was to see how fast he could go up the side of the house and into the back yard. One day due to an error of judgment he managed to demolish the toilet. Luckily it was unoccupied.

In those days you didn't have to do much wrong to be sent to Borstal. The final straw came for Colin when he untruthfully told a friend's mother that her son had given him permission to use her son's 500 Ariel motorbike while he was away doing his eighteen-year old Army training. After riding it for some time Colin was finally arrested by the police, and this along with numerous unpaid traffic fines led to him being given a term in Borstal. I was quite keen on Colin's sister Lois, and asked her out, but on our first date, while riding down Colombo Street we saw another guy I knew by the name of Ricky and he turned to follow us. After trying to lose him down Colombo Street by speeding I could see he wanted to talk to me so pulled over and he stopped beside me and we exchanged pleasantries. Then he said to Lois, "Don't go out with that mad bugger, he will kill you!"

Next thing I knew he was going out with her himself and ended up marrying her, making Colin his brother-in-law.

Shortly afterwards, Ricky bought his first car. It was a 1936 Chevrolet Coupe, which had four bald tyres. He asked me if I would like go with him on a trip to Invercargill to the Borstal to visit Colin. The car was really only a two-seater, but Ricky had invited his future mother-in-law, also Lois his soon-to-be wife and her brother Wayne, and to compensate for the lack of seating, he removed the shelf between the front seats and the back window and put a mattress in the boot. So after work one wintry Friday, we all piled in and started out for Invercargill. We only got as far as Burnham when we had to slow down because there was a traffic accident ahead. It was dark, but we saw a Mark One Zephyr upside down on the roadside, and people lying on the roadside covered in blankets. We stopped to see what was happening, and found the road so slippery you could hardly stand up on it because it was covered in black ice, which had been caused by a pine plantation sheltering the road from the sun all day long.

In those days the speed limit was only fifty miles per hour on the open road, and with numerous small towns to pass through at thirty, Ricky became tired and he said to me, "You can drive now." It was a bit like my first motorbike all over again, as I had never driven a car in my life! But I knew the basics, and drove carefully. We were getting along quite nicely, until I came to a downhill stretch of road, where I realized we were on a sheet of ice. I pushed the gear lever through to second gear, and released the clutch, whereupon I immediately went into a slide, and we fishtailed down the road. Every time I tried to correct it I over-corrected, and the fishtail got worse. I was convinced we were about to do a 180-degree turn and face the way we had come, when as quickly as it started, it finished when it suddenly bit in to a bit of frost-free road and straightened up. No one said anything but it certainly gave me a fright and made me even more careful.

After driving all night we arrived at Invercargill at the doors of the Borstal about eight a.m., only to find that visiting hours weren't until the afternoon, so we had to go away again and we drove down to Bluff for a ride. On the way Ricky tried the car out for top speed and found it was only seventy miles per hour. We were lucky he didn't blow it up the way he thrashed it. After visiting Colin that afternoon, we started out again for home. I had had no sleep at all since Thursday night and neither had Ricky, and he drove until he couldn't drive any longer, then asked me to drive. By that time, it was Saturday evening and I drove as far as just past Timaru, when I realized we needed more petrol and we would have to turn back to Timaru to get some. I tried to do a U-turn on the road, and ended up with the front in the gutter, put the car into reverse, let the clutch out, and went straight to sleep and backed into the gutter on the other side of the road. This woke me up with a start. It woke Ricky too, and I told him I could not drive any further. He tried to convince me otherwise, but there was no way I could carry on to Christchurch so Ricky took over once more.

The next thing I remember was waking up with bright lights shining in my face and how quiet it was. We had run out of petrol in Hagley Avenue near the hospital, and Ricky had hired a taxi and gone to get some.

Ricky worked at the Christchurch Tile Company and convinced me to leave my job at Urlwins and work with him at the tile factory where the money was much better. A married man on reasonably good wages in those days was making about twelve pounds a week, and we could make twenty pounds a week and be finished early by about two p.m. There was a flat rate for a certain number of tiles, we were both good hard workers with a good work ethic, times were good and there was virtually no unemployment. We were working six days a week at the tile company. Ricky, who could never get enough work, became the foreman at the starch products factory near the Ferrymead Bridge, and we both worked there on the 4.00 p.m. to midnight shift seven days a week. One night I made a mistake when we had a machinery breakdown. I went up into the loft where bags of flour were stored and sat down for a minute. It was very warm and I was dead tired and dropped off to sleep. The first thing I knew, I was woken with a jet of water and there stood Ricky with a bicycle-pump full of water squirting me in the face. It woke me up all right, and I was soon conscious again.

Ricky, who was a workaholic, wasn't satisfied just working the equivalent of thirteen full-time days in every seven without a break, he wanted more, so he bought himself an electric welder and started making trailers from home. Every day he would race home from the tile company, and immediately start work on his trailers, which he never stopped producing until he left New Zealand for Australia sometime in the 1970s.

We became good friends and later next-door neighbours when we became married men with families.

ARMY DAYS

In those days every male aged eighteen in New Zealand had to register for the Army. Eventually my time came to go to Burnham to do my twelve weeks of basic training. I thought I was so clever,

I was going to have my friends come out and pick me up at night, to cruise around town on our motorbikes or so I thought, then deliver me back so I would be there in the morning, but little did I know the Army wasn't that stupid. On the day of our arrival at Burnham, all the conscripts were separated into different groups, and sent off to different locations that same day. Our group was told we were to be engineers and were shipped off to Linton near Palmerston North that very morning. We were taken by train to the ferry and sailed from Lyttelton Harbour to Wellington. We were given only enough time to phone our families to say we would be passing the main central Station at Christchurch if they wanted to call in and say goodbye.

At Linton, we stayed in four-man huts; one of my hut mates also from Christchurch was Dennis Adair. He, like I, was keen on motorbikes so he talked me into having a go at scrambles when we finally returned to Christchurch. They worked us really hard at Linton, and by the end of the twelve-week period we were fitter than we had ever been in our lives. The final week we were there we were taken out on a night exercise, and marched from the camp into the hills and I volunteered to carry a Bren gun, as well as a pack, a shovel or pick stuffed down between your pack and your back and also a couple of bandoliers of ammunition. That was a mistake.

We were supposed to assemble a Bailey bridge in the dark, with booms and bangs and explosions and all sorts of noises simulating a war going on all around us. After assembling our bridge, our sergeant was leading us off somewhere, still in the dark. I became separated from the rest of our team at about two a.m. and found myself a warm spot in the bush under some ferns to have a rest. At first light I went in search of my unit, and came across other units and asked if they knew where my group was. Eventually I found them and was made to feel a lot better when I found the person in charge of our group had also become lost.

For about three years after our training we all had to do an annual camp for two weeks at Tekapo and live under canvas. It was very cold, and the weather was unusually inclement. It certainly didn't compare with Linton and the warmth of the four-man huts. The food at Linton is worth a mention and I remember writing home to my girlfriend telling her about the various insects and critters found in our meals. Wasps stuck in the jam and honey, caterpillars and slugs in the lettuce, and flies and other unappetizing things, were found in our tea, which was a funny purple colour, but we were so hard worked and hungry that no one ever complained. You just pushed those objects to one side and enjoyed the meals. Even with those additives the food was always good. When I came home to my mother's wonderful cooking after being in the army I didn't find it as good as I had remembered, and found myself preferring the plainer meals given to us in the army.

In 1957 I married my teenage sweetheart, Val, at the young age of nineteen, and we had a son Glen, the first of our three children. We later had two girls, Jill and Linda. Life was busy and we both worked full-time jobs to provide a home for our young family.

LIFE AS AN ANIMAL CONTROL OFFICER

For twenty years I was employed by the Christchurch City Council as an Animal Control Officer. During this time we tried various combinations of work hours to provide service to the public twenty four hours a day, seven days a week. My work was varied and interesting. There was always something happening. One morning at three a.m. for example, there were three horses creating a traffic hazard right by a bend on the road by the Kiwi Bacon factory in Maces Rd. The police had cornered them, but the horses were spooked because the police kept shining their torches in their faces. As soon

I arrived I asked them to turn their torches off and the horses quietened down and were able to be returned to the nearby paddock from which they had escaped.

Being on call for twelve hours overnight, you never knew what was going to happen. Sometimes we were called out to help the Police and restrain dogs while they raided houses for drugs. We were constantly dealing with upset people who didn't want their dogs impounded, and we regularly had to deal with attacking dogs and people who had been bitten. Sometimes we had to sort out cattle on the road. A large bull would regularly escape from a paddock in Spencerville, even though he had a chain in his nose, which he had to drag with him everywhere he went. A black bull on a black night is a bad combination.

One night I picked up the big black bull up from Spencerville. I first had to go back to the pound to collect the big double horse float. On the way back, the size of the bull caused the whole trailer to rock and roll, and I knew I would have to impound him in pens at the City Council Sewerage Farm which adjoined the dog pound. It was ten o'clock at night and Rex was still up, so he came with me to put the bull away. We took him down and put him in a pen and both remarked at how big he was.

Early next morning I received a call from Rex, who every morning walked his Greyhounds through the Sewage Farm. He said "You won't believe it, but that bull has gone!

In the meantime Tony Childs, the manager of the sewage farm, arrived as we were looking around for the bull. There were paddocks full of black bulls but none anywhere near the size of the one we had impounded the night before. It wasn't long before we discovered him. He was between a five-strand barbed wire fence, and the back of a large implement shed. He walked along the backside of the shed and he was so large the staples that held the fence were flying out. We drove him around back into the cattle yards and we got him back in the yards where he again escaped while we were watching. The cattle yard fences were five foot six high, but the bull just reared up and slid over the fence like a huge black eel.

The owners were soon looking for the bull. They took him away and removed him from the Spencerville area entirely so he was no longer a problem.

My fellow employees and I worked in pairs, and were supposed to share the workload by taking every second call out during after hours, but it was sometimes difficult, as we lived several miles apart, and so we were more inclined to cover the areas closer to home ourselves, even though it wasn't our turn. Quite often you would be out on one call when another would come in. Rather than disturb our workmates we would just go to the next emergency rather than call them out for the job. Some nights there would be nothing much happening, and other nights would be hectic, with no sleep at all. Many a time I had just got back into bed when another call came through and I would have to go back out to work.

With roaming dogs, the first thing we had to do was to try and catch the dog so we could impound it and prevent other people being attacked. Then we had to obtain a statement from the complainant, any witnesses, and the dog's owners if they could be found. Obtaining statements was very time consuming.

The police often asked us to help them when they were searching houses for drugs. If there were dogs on the property we would take them away out of danger while they did their work.

Dealing with biting dogs made up a lot of the work. One Sunday morning I was called out because of a dog attack. I was shocked when I saw the complainant. The young man had just discharged himself from hospital. Tragically his nose had been completely bitten off by his friend's bull terrier! It was not the first time we had complaints about that dog so he had to be disposed of.

Once I was waiting to finish my shift at seven in the morning, when I had another call out. A large Rottweiler had knocked an elderly man to the ground on his own property. Apparently he had looked out his kitchen window, and noticed the dog in his enclosed back yard, and went to open the gate to let it out, the dog jumped up on him and knocked him the ground. When I arrived there was no dog to be seen. I found it was behind his garage in a small enclosed area which had been fenced off to form a pen to house a German-Shepherd bitch in season. The man had not told me this!

So there were two dogs in the pen, the Rottweiler and the bitch in season. The Rottweiler intent on protecting the bitch rushed at me. I had the loop on my catch pole fully extended in preparation, but the noose would barely fit over the dogs head, because he was so large. He was the biggest Rottweiler I had ever seen, and I have seen a few!

I managed after a struggle to capture him, and once he was caught he was very good and tried to tow me out of the section. The dog was impounded and completely filled one side of the dog van. When the owners claimed him, they told me that they had weighed him, and he was 16 stone (102kg)! He really was a nice dog, fortunately for the elderly man, not vicious at all. I found most Rottweilers were very good. They are intelligent, and not naturally nasty unless trained to be.

On one call out not far from home, I was told that a woman had a blocked sewer, but the drain layers refused to work there because they were afraid of the neighbour's big Rottweiler. So I went there to have a word with the dog's owner, and found there was more to the story that met the eye. The property with the dog had a fence which ran from the side of house across to the boundary fence, and he claimed their dog had not been out the front. When I got back to work I was told there had been another complaint which had involved the police, and a person doing gardening on the dog owner's property had been severely bitten, needing stitches in his arm and leg. Mark Vincent, my boss asked me to go and pick up the dog and bring it back to the pound. As I left, he said, "Get the owners to put it in the truck themselves". I dismissed the idea thinking I could just handle it myself.

But when I knocked on the door I couldn't see the dog anywhere, and a slightly built young lady answered the door. She invited me into the house, told me the dog belonged to her husband, but she had registered it in her name because he was always in jail so she was legally the owner. She asked me if it was ok to feed the dog before I took him away. I said yes, and she took me out into the back yard and opened the side door on the garage and let the dog onto the enclosed back yard where we both were. The dog obviously hungry gulped down the dog roll, plastic and all, all the time with its eyes fixed on me, and mine fixed on him!

Just as he was cleaning up the last of the roll the woman's baby started crying inside the house and she went off to tend to the child and left me with the dog. Suddenly he came straight at me barking and snarling, dodging and ducking in and out trying to bite. All I had in my hand was a short dog chain with a leather strap on one end and a clip on the other. As he kept lunging and snapping at me, I had my left arm across the front of me, for protection, and he tore a hunk out of the sleeve of my nylon jacket. In the meantime the dog's owner came running and screaming out of the house and luckily for me the dog had a collar on. The female owner grabbed him by the collar and fell on the ground under him. This enabled me, once the dog took its eye off me, to grab the collar myself, and I screwed it up tight choking a bit of the wind out of him.

"Whatever you do, don't let go," I told the lady. We frog-marched him out to the back of the van. I took him to the pound where he was put down immediately.

I once tried to catch a couple of dogs outside some shops (one was a bitch in season). When I called her she wagged her tail and wanted to come to me, but the dog tried to protect her by getting between us, snarling and showing his teeth. I decided to ignore them and they were running backwards and forwards amongst people on the footpath. As the dog passed me I hooked two fingers in his collar whereupon he immediately twisted around and sunk his teeth into my wrist. The dog ended up with my left arm rammed hard down his throat and my left knee across his throat, while my right hand held his back legs in the air keeping him on his back. He knew he was beaten, but my big problem was getting the lead – a piece of sash cord – from my pocket to put around his neck. Nobody stopped to help except for one elderly gentleman who asked if he could assist. I asked him to take the sash cord from my pocket which he did, but it was tangled. He had trouble unravelling it, all the while my wrist was bleeding into the dog's mouth. I had to explain what to do, but the gentleman feared the dog might bite him. I pointed out that couldn't happen with my hand down his throat. Eventually we got there and I lead the dog away and put it in the van. I was quite surprised a few days later when the council received a letter from the elderly gentleman who was a Salvation Army officer from the area, saying how he had assisted the dog ranger who had used very mild expletives but would have been quite justified had he used much stronger language!

One dog, a Corgi, took a fancy to me even though I had impounded him twice, and the owner, a solo mother, couldn't afford to get him back a third time. I was reluctant to imprison him again, because I knew he would probably not be released. If he saw me in the street he would race up to me and wanted to get in the van. Probably no one else ever took any notice of him! So I would pick him up and take him for a ride with me for the day and would drop him off at his gate at the end of my shift. He was quite happy to go inside after that. I never knew what eventually became of him, but he was a nice old dog.

It's illegal to exercise dogs in a cemetery. One day I spotted a man running his dogs around the graves. He saw me coming and quickly put his dogs in the car and took off in a hurry. Unfortunately for him I got his car registration which in those days we could check out on the spot. I found out his home address. I arrived at his house five minutes behind him. There were no dogs registered at that address, and I wanted to talk to him about exercising the dogs in the graveyard. After persistent knocking, he finally answered the door. I found out that I knew who he was. He had come upon hard times. He had no job and needed all his money for his alcohol. He became quite upset and begged me to let him go. I told him I couldn't do that because it was more than my job was worth, so I told him that if I registered his dogs for him, he would have to keep the registration up in the future. He agreed to that. I did help out one or two people a few times in that way, as I genuinely had a soft spot for people who loved their dogs and cared for them even when they came upon difficult times

In the days when it was legal to keep ferrets, Rex the pound keeper had a few which he kept in cages. He told me to keep my eyes open for a white ferret which he had lost. There were numerous rabbits around the pound, so the ferret would not have gone hungry. I think it had been missing for a week or more, when while putting a stray dog into one of the outside pens around midnight one night, the ferret suddenly appeared in the pen with the dog. It had come from the next pen over and walked underneath the dog's belly. Not being experienced with ferrets, I put my hand down for it to sniff, like you would with a dog, and it took my hand in its mouth very gently, but its teeth were like razor blades, and it sliced the back of my hand, drawing blood.

I grabbed a coat from Rex's truck, and wrapped the ferret in it before picking it up and placed him on the front seat of the vehicle. Next morning I rang Rex to tell him where the ferret was. He was pleased to get him back, even though the little beast had pooped in the front of his truck and cleaned up a whole cake of chocolate which he had stolen from the glove box!

I enjoyed my working life as an animal control officer, it was varied and interesting. But even more so, my pig-hunting days were even more exciting. Looking back now, I would not change a thing.

TOP: My parents Guy and Nan Broadhurst with Lorna and me. BOTTOM: The five-a-side hockey team. Bruce Berkley, Maurice Berkley, Warwick Broadhurst, Gerald Deavol, and Peter Durant.

TOP: Me and Colin Hurrell. Bikes are a 1949 AJS7R 500cc with BSA motor and a 1954 Velocete 350. BOTTOM: My son Glen on my 1951 Norton International, and his cousin Neil and my 1939 Triumph.

TOP: Family. First wife Val, and children Linda, Glen, Jill and me seated.
BOTTOM: Me on my 1939 Triumph 500 at a hill climb event at Heathcote.

EARLY MEMORIES

Bee and me.

www.ingramcontent.com/pod-product-compliance
Lightning Source LLC
Chambersburg PA
CBHW071356290426
44108CB00014B/1565